The Last Roman Catholic ?

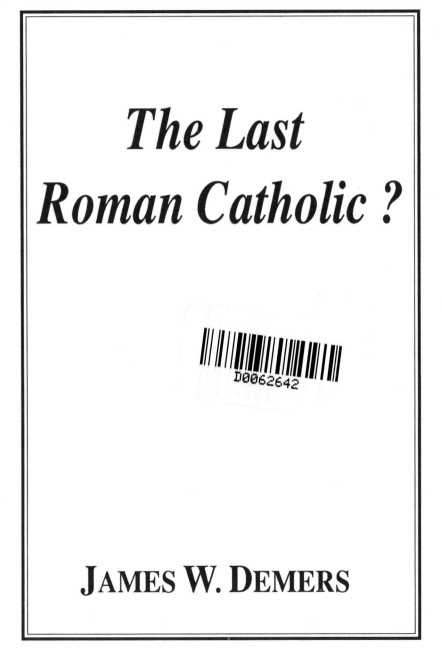

D0062642

JAMES W. DEMERS

Published by
Creative Bound Inc.
P.O. Box 424, Carp, Ontario
Canada K0A 1L0

ISBN 0-921165-17-X
Printed and bound in Canada

First Printing   October 1991
Second Printing   January 1992
Third Printing   April 1992

Editor: Catherine Marjoribanks
Design and Art Direction by Creative Bound Inc.
Cover Photo by Dave Andrews, Andrews-Newton Photography
Ltd., Ottawa, Ontario

Canadian Cataloguing in Publication Data

Demers, James, 1942-
     The Last Roman Catholic ?

Includes bibliographical references.
ISBN 0-921165-17-X

     1. Catholic Church--History--1965- . 2. Catholic
Church--Controversial literature. I. Title.

BX1779.5.D35 1991   282'.09'045   C91-090387-5

Dedication

to
Irene
whose
name
means
"Peace"

It is as if the treasures of the Faith

all over North America were simply dropped into the

hands of those who hated Roman Catholicism.

To understand how that could happen one need

look no further than the

capital city of Canada

in 1988-1989.

Table of Contents

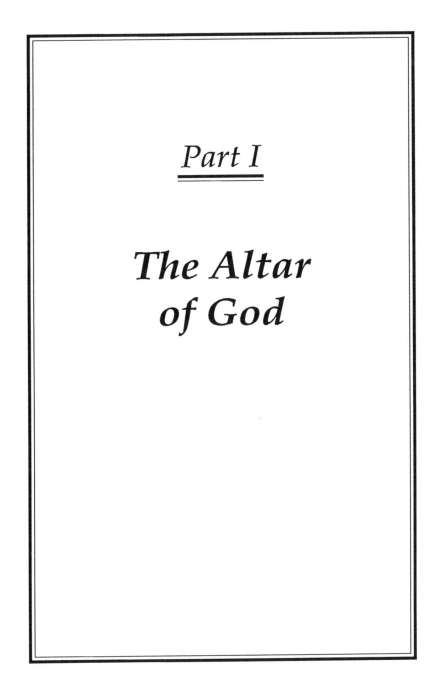

Part I

The Altar
of God

1

Saints Along The River

Soon after arriving in the archdiocese of Ottawa in June of 1988, I located a favourite geographical reference point that would, in days to come, serve as a sort of wisdom stone to which I would often go to ponder the state of the world and, in particular, the state of the Church that I so dearly love.

It was the rocky promontory of Nepean Point, a high ledge of earth on which stands a grand statue of Samuel de Champlain looking westward over the country he explored and the river he employed to do so, the Ottawa.

When the French first charted this river, they named each rapids and waterfall after a saint, in the order of honour they hold in Roman Catholicism's Litany of the Saints. This converted the voyageurs' difficult river journey to the heartland into a procession accompanied by a litany of water and stone that reinforced in each voyageur the courage needed to go on.

The river was the means of bringing the faith inland. Spires punctuating horizons on both sides of the river were sufficient in number to enliven the hopes of a middle-aged Catholic who had come to Ottawa in the summer of 1988 to seek out his spiritual heritage. Yet there were signs that summer that such a search might actually be too late.

On Nepean Point, between Champlain's rock and Sussex Drive, the brand new National Gallery of Canada had recently opened to the acclaim of an enraptured public with an exhibition of the works of Degas. If, while unfolding a city map on the crowded gallery esplanade that summer, you asked passers-by the identity and location of nearby Catholic churches, you might very well have been asked, "Have you heard about the Oratorians?"

The name identified a major *cause célèbre* making daily headlines in the city papers. "The Oratorian affair" had to do with a group of nine Roman Catholic priests and Brothers who had become the focus of a heated letter-writing campaign between a certain group of the laity in the archdiocese of Ottawa and the archbishop of that archdiocese, one Joseph Aurèle Plourde.

The very day of my arrival in Ottawa, the Superior of the Oratorians had made the paper, pictured on the steps of St. Brigid's, the church where he and some fellow priests and Brothers had for one year been conducting their lives according to the regimen of the Oratory of St. Philip Neri.

An Oratory is simply a place of prayer. St. Philip founded the first Congregation of the Oratory in Rome in 1575. The capital of Christendom at that time was, by all accounts, wild and wicked. A good-humoured, good-hearted, cordial and witty man, Neri saw that what the Church was lacking was holiness. He decided to combat the corruption of the day with simple piety, purity of heart and natural, unaffected gaiety. In his burning desire to make souls receptive to God, he placed great value on music and the arts.

When Pope Gregory XIII gave Neri and his followers a run-down church in 1575, they restored it.[1] Resisting the temptation to establish a new order, Neri and his followers determined to simply remain united by mutual love and for the common purpose of bringing souls to God through prayer, preaching and the sacraments. The reform of the Church in that era owes a great deal to those first Oratorians.

Of all the other Oratorians to follow, the most well known is Neri's nineteenth- century admirer and imitator, John Henry Cardinal Newman, who founded an Oratory in Birmingham in 1848.[2] Closer to home, an Oratory has been thriving in Toronto throughout the 1970s and '80s. Now, according to the headlines, there was one in Ottawa.

Directly across from the esplanade on Sussex Drive stands the basilica of Notre Dame. It is spectacularly fitting that visitors to the National Gallery of Canada should be able to cross the street and view the interior of this great church. Notre Dame is the perfect reminder that throughout the centuries the Church has been the single greatest patron of artistic excellence in art, music and architecture.

The interior of Notre Dame is a treasury of gilt-edged shapes and shadows reflecting Roman Catholic worship as it has existed over the last few hundred years. Within Notre Dame, the Catholic finds evidence of a cherished past lovingly preserved.

Mid-sanctuary stands a massive main altar, the centre piece a veritable catechism in sculpted figures. Rising tier upon tier are patriarchs, prophets, the Nativity, Jesus teaching, the Resurrection, Christ giving the keys to Peter, the Ascension, Christ enthroned and crowned, the nine choirs of angels, apostles, evangelists, the busts of Peter and Paul, sixteen Fathers and Doctors of the Church, sixteen Founders of Religious Orders and, to keep them all in line, forty angels.

Light from stained-glass windows highlights with mauves, blues, greens and gold the faces, gestures and moments of salvation history that are the bedrock principles of Catholic faith: the Decalogue, *Pater Noster* and Creed.

To be Roman Catholic means one accepts as teaching authority on these principles the Church of Rome, with the Pope at its head.

I have remained Roman in my Catholicity all my life because from the first day I ever heard of Rome and St. Peter's I knew that it was home. That feeling has not diminished to this day.

Standing in Notre Dame contemplating the spectacle, one can easily conclude it was no accident that the First Commandment came first: "I am the Lord thy God, thou shall not have strange Gods before me." The success of the Church for nineteen centuries has risen from its ability to defend God's claim to authority over us.

For those nineteen centuries, with art, architecture, music, vestments and ritual, the point was made that *we are created.* That God created man. That God is greater than man, separate and unique from us. The Church has steadfastly refused to accommodate the notion that if we get smart enough we will be like Him, or that we happened somehow on our own — in other words, that man *is* God.

From the first days of the Church, sacred art, music and architecture served a specific role: the heart was filled, the soul was uplifted, the intellect transformed into its purest state, a receptor for truths about the Creator. Over all those centuries, the Church was to continuously express that the most important fact of human life is that it is not meant to end here, and that the all-powerful God willingly allowed His Son to be pinned to a tree so we could earn eternal life.

The central act of worship re-enacting that great salvation drama was the mass. With reverential ritual, sights and sounds, the mass expressed what man might not: awe, wonder and gratitude that the Son of God would go to His own death, then Resurrect Himself to show His authority over Death and over our destiny.

That climax of salvation history, the death and Resurrection of the Son of God, determines the shape, sights and sounds of worship services for every Christian denomination on earth. Schisms, reformations, rebellions and revolutions have not changed that. But for the Roman Catholic, there is one specific belief at the very heart of this prayer, the mass, that separates and sets him apart from all others, namely, that the Son of God is truly present at it, that His great sacrifice of love is truly repeated in each mass, and that we are invited in each instance to eat His actual flesh and drink His actual blood.

At stake in the Oratorian affair was nothing less than the very survival of this belief.

The church that housed the Oratorians stands in Lowertown, in the heart of old Ottawa, a mere seven hundred paces from Notre Dame. For one hundred years it has nourished the hopes and dreams of those non-French-speaking Lowertown families once referred to as "Irish and Others."[3] In

1888, the non-French-speaking parishioners from Notre Dame pressured Archbishop Duhamel for a separate church. They named it St. Brigid's after Ireland's second-most-famous saint.

It is a church you might have passed a hundred times in your own city, a massive edifice in the oldest, most run-down part of town. It was built to last, to serve the poor, that class of which every city in the world has an endless supply. It is the kind of church that manages over the years somehow to remain upright and constant while all around the world sheds its skin, grows another, sheds it again. There is one like it in every province, state, country of the world. Its baptismal records tell the history of a people. For the duration of the Oratorians' tenure it was known as the Ottawa Oratory, although later, the archbishop would claim, on a technicality, that there had never been an Oratory in Ottawa.

The week of my first visit to the Ottawa Oratory, a scaffolding surrounded the altar and filled the sanctuary to the high ceiling. A restoration was underway, stripping off decades of dust and grey paint. As it did, it revealed the muted greens and gold-and-white of the original decor which, seen through the crisscrossing orange pipes of the scaffolding, caused images of Irish history to dance in the mind.

It was also, coincidentally, the same week that in Econe, Switzerland, Archbishop Marcel Lefebvre faced the crucial test of his obedience to Rome. The confrontation boiled down to one single issue and one single event. Lefebvre refused to abandon the Tridentine mass, the "mass of the ages" formalized at the Council of Trent 1545-63. Of the new mass, the Novus Ordo of Paul VI, simplified, streamlined and in the vernacular, Lefebvre said it was the product of another conception of the Catholic religion, in fact, a product of another religion.[4] He described the Pauline innovation with the unfortunate words "the bastard mass." Attempts by Paul VI and John Paul II to reconcile Lefebvre to Rome had failed and a schism loomed. In Econe, Switzerland, Lefebvre had scheduled the consecration of new bishops for June 30. If he proceeded, he would be excommunicated.

The importance of the outcome of that day must have

been in the minds of many Catholics as they made their way to St. Brigid's for mass on Sunday, July 3. Perhaps that was what heightened the senses. Or perhaps it was the sight of the parishioners kneeling in hushed silence, awaiting the beginning of mass, that seemed to sharpen perceptions. The solemnity, blessedly silent, outlawed time. Every action and image was immediate and free of pretension.

A bell rings, people rise, the procession begins. Fourteen altar boys in cassock and surplice, and leading the way, a tall, angelic young man carrying the censor from which rises wafts of incense. The altar boys walk slowly past with a careful, measured pace, as though stepping into wildflowers, cautious, deliberate, feet selecting each step so as not to crush the petals of something perfect. Shoes weigh against the polished surface of the antique aisle, pressing down gently as though paying homage to the tree that gave it wood. They approach the altar of God. Behind them comes the priest in chasuble and alb. It is the Superior, Father William Ashley, recognizable from the newspaper clipping. But that is unusual, that vestment. Albs and chasubles have long since gone to rummage sales.

That cannot be incense. Those amber crystals must be something else — shattered remnants from all the stained-glass windows that will never see again — but not incense.

In the choir gallery above, a voice intones the Introit. The sounds, sights, pace are all reverential. The curtain has just risen on a vital act in a theatre of prayer. Can any drama match this? Man, with humility, keeping an appointment with his Creator, to acknowledge his limitations and give thanks for being raised above all other nature.

The altar is reached. Incense rises. Something greater than ourselves will soon be here. Praises are intoned. Faults admitted. Mercy sought. Much more than a close encounter will happen soon. A goodness, so great only a child could imagine it, is coming to scatter darkness, for God is brighter than the sun and has no shadow.

"*Kyrie Eleison ... Christe Eleison ... Gloria ... Credo in unum Deum,*" the choir sings.

Much has been made of the validity of emotion in prayer. I have always been suspicious of it, for the simple reason that faith must survive within us even when emotions are dead. I have never experienced any rush of the Holy Spirit, nor do I have any inclination to be "born again." But that first day at the Ottawa Oratory, one single moment elevated me far outside and above myself and instantly provided an overview of the faith I had not had before.

"Et Incarnatus Est ..." the choir sang as a hush consumed the interior of St. Brigid's and the congregation went down on its knees. Here, in an act of devotion more reverent than any I had witnessed in twenty years, was the truth of the Incarnation brought home with innocent simplicity, and I was a shepherd on my knees at the door of the stable once more before my new-born king. Of all the achievements of the Oratorians during their tenure at St. Brigid's, none will ever surpass for me that single moment. They had brought me back to the manger.

Yes, that fragrance, it was incense.

The orange scaffolding stretched toward the sanctuary ceiling, as if carried upward by the clouds billowing from the altar boy's censor. High above, the outline of a mural was being redefined, nursed back into the light of day after decades under grey. And surrounding the scaffold, the original wood of the sanctuary walls was being called back from latex exile. Shafts of coloured light with tone and shape reached in from the stained-glass windows to play in the rising clouds of incense and tell surprising stories. Colour was re-emerging everywhere. A restoration by loving hands was slowly returning the interior to its original splendour. Under the Oratorians, glimpses of the original late-Victorian designs were, little by little, being led forward into the present, and it was possible for the eye to show obedience once more to the architect's concept. A work of great sensitivity and skill was unfolding here.

Spend a week asking people what was at the root of the Oratorian affair and you will get a month of answers. Ask them twelve times over and you will notice something spectacularly odd — namely, that in a year when priests and

Brothers were being arrested by the dozen in Canada for unspeakable acts committed against youths in their trust, the Oratorians, who endured two years of relentless public scrutiny and battering, could not be tainted by any accusation even hinting of moral scandal.

The Oratorian affair was a wide-open conflict between two forces at work in the Church today. Those two forces have been in conflict in the Church throughout its entire history in varying degrees but have polarized into two diametrically opposed ideologies since the 1960s and Vatican II. On one side are those who think of themselves as progressives and see themselves as the hope of the modern Church, the champions of individual conscience. On the other side is that force best described by Pius X in 1907: "The conserving force in the Church is Tradition and Tradition is represented by religious authority."[5] The Oratorians were caught for two years in the white heat of naked public conflict because they exemplified this conserving force.

The Oratorians, orthodox and traditional, were dedicated to relying on all the Church has had to offer for two thousand years to protect and promote the reality of Christ's actual presence, not only at the centre of Catholicism but right there on the tongue of all who received him.

Inevitably, the Oratorians were categorized as a remote minority, as reactionaries, extremists and, of course, fanatics, by those so-called Progressives who believed that in distancing themselves from the core beliefs of Catholicism, from tradition and from the authority of Rome, they represented the majority of Catholics. The Progressives openly and aggressively promoted the question "What will become of the Church if we allow ourselves to be dragged back into the dark ages?" and branded the Oratorians' form of prayer and worship "outdated spirituality."

The conflict reached into every aspect of the faith, but at the very centre of the tug-of-war was the mass. What it truly meant, what it actually said, how it was actually conducted, who was officiating and who was offering it were all at stake. Dependent on the outcome was nothing less than the survival or the destruction of the priesthood.

2

Tradition Has It

An age of terrorism dawned in the Church in the years of the Second Vatican Council and its aftermath. The battle for the mass — to Catholics the final battle — began in earnest. Rules and laws taken for granted as the very means by which mankind would survive became the exact same means by which dissenters could do violence to a great portion of mankind. Minorities could terrorize simply by devaluing the laws designed to safeguard the majority. What could be simpler?

Those who would hijack the mass had first to devalue it, if they could. They could not have expected it to be so easy. The hijackers slipped on board under cover of a password — "*aggiornamento.*"

The word came innocently enough from everyone's favourite Roman, the man with the turned-down nose and ingratiating smile, Angelo Giuseppe Roncalli, Pope John XXIII. Some would say his appeal was based on the long-overdue need for change or bringing up to date that *aggiornamento* means; others claim he would have had a profound effect on any era. There was about him that universal purity of character and intent that Catholics and non-Catholics alike find in Francis of Assisi. Certainly, Roncalli appealed not only to non-Catholics but to non-Christians as well.

The Protestants made a great deal of John XXIII, some even calling him "ours" and "the Protestants' Pope." I liked him too, for a lot of reasons, not the least of which was that he made life with my Protestant friends easier.

I was unsettled, however, by the fact that we saw more of him in pictures and television in a short year than we ever saw of Pius XII in the whole of the '50s. What did that all mean? I used to worry about that even then, without ever really imagining what television was about to do to the Church. I was unsettled also by his nose, which was very much like my father's, drooping down at one end. It accomplished for him what it accomplished for my father, emphasizing an ingratiating grin that could make you forgive him absolutely anything and everything.

To say that with Vatican II John XXIII turned the Church upside-down sounds so trite now. Yet, if you held a global satellite quiz show with contestants from all over the world, chances are the question "What was Pope John XXIII famous for?" would have participants from Tibet, Tierra del Fuego, Tristan de Cunha, Tallahassee and Calabogie diving for their buzzers to register that answer, " He turned the Church upside-down."

His intention was pure enough: "To return the Church to the simple form it possessed when it left the hand of Jesus Christ, its founder."[1] I have never understood how anyone could even think that was possible. Is that not a lot like me saying to my calculus teacher that I would sit out exams until trigonometry was returned to the simple form it possessed when the rock left David's sling for Goliath's forehead? Nevertheless, John XXIII did talk like that, about simplifying things, and overnight the name Galilee returned to our vocabulary, and a million angry young men beat their swords into folk guitars and began reworking the Sermon on the Mount.

History will covet the two highlights of John XXIII's mythology — he charmed the world, he threw a party.

The Second Vatican Council was a surprise to all when it was announced, not least because of the simple fact that ninety-nine out of every one hundred Catholics were not even aware there had been a First. Keeping track of such things was not part of the make-up of the ordinary Catholic, who had spent the last ninety years since the First Vatican Council thankful just to have popes who were admirable, intelligent, respected and strong enough to make their will and the will of the Church known without having to assemble the troops. From all reports it seems Vatican II was a surprise even to Pope John himself, who was quite forthcoming in admitting that he had spent next to no time at all thinking about it. This innocent candour simply amplified the glow his persona was spreading across the globe.

But the underlying assumption that all of this was great good fortune of a never before heard-of or dreamed-of variety was disconcerting to me even then. On the small front porch bookshelf, where my older brothers and sisters sought out relief from mid-week or Sunday afternoon boredom, there, among the raggedy-eared volumes on the lives of the saints, John of the Cross, Teresa of Avila and the avalanche of pamphlets on The Little Flower, was a history of the Popes.

So I knew that John XXIII had no monopoly on simplicity. Long before him came the saintly Pius VII, a man so dignified he drew sympathy even from the chilled heart of the artist of the French Revolution, David. Pius VII was taken prisoner by Napoleon and, as though to demolish the pretensions of his jailer's million and one future biographers and historians, Pius referred to him, from beginning to end, simply as "My son."[2]

Then there was Pius IX, pope of the First Vatican Council, who, with his simple formula *"Tolerare per vivere,"* uttered when the papal states were abolished in 1870, provided an undying motto to the oppressed everywhere: "Tolerate in order to go on living."[3]

There, on that crowded bookshelf, I found evidence of the common touch in none other than the elegant and eloquent Leo XIII, who was not afraid to reveal his all-too-human pessimism when he said, of the century about to yield to this one, "If the Good Lord permits such a century as this to repeat itself mankind might not survive."[4]

There too I read, and, I think, heard the sigh of Pius X,

who remarked, upon seeing a Sanpietrini adjust the descent of Leo XIII's coffin by broadsiding it with a hearty kick, "Popes, like everyone else, are of no consequence when they pass from this life."[5]

Pius X, the man labelled "a peasant elevated to the papacy,"[6] was, if God does use the simple to confound the wise, the right man in the right place at the right time. Even his critics called him a man of goodness and simplicity. He became parish priest to the world in the years leading up to the First World War. It was left to him to identify, in his September 7, 1907, encyclical *Pascendi Domenici Gregis*, the new system of theology threatening the Church. He called it Modernism.

As Francis Murphy outlines in *The Papacy Today*, Modernists used all the popular buzz-words so cherished by Europeans breaking out from under centuries of monarchical rule: "conscience," "conciliation," "autonomy," "liberation," "revival." But their call for change extended to the primacy of human conscience, conciliation between liberty and authority, the autonomy of science, the liberation of the Church from superfluous ecclesiastical structure, revision of the liturgy and a break with the past, proposing that Christian philosophy need no longer be rooted in medieval scholasticism — all of this promoted through the ever-expanding publishing enterprises of university presses at the turn of the century.[7]

Those who would overthrow the Church always publish more books for public library shelves than those who would save her. But the overwhelming majority of Catholic faithful do not spend all their time between book covers, which, if one were to believe all the superstar philosophers, theologians, historians, critics and reformers bound there, was the only way a rational Catholic at the turn of the century could ever learn what the Church must do to be meaningful and relevant. And so the overwhelming majority of Catholic faithful did not know that for the Church to be meaningful, relevant, it must scrap scholastic philosophy, demolish the authority of the Church and dismantle the magisterium, the teaching authority of the Church.

Pius X saw the Modernist movement as an attempt to

break papal authority, to destroy the absolute character of
Catholic truth and called it "watered-down Catholicism."[8] A
tough pope for tough times, Pius X defeated the Modernists
with the very weapon they wished to disarm: the full might of
papal authority. The same once-untouchable theologians who
accused the Pope of pamphleteering against their freedom of
expression now filled even more library shelves with
condemnations of Pius X that are little more than spite-filled
volumes of graffiti.

There too, at my mother's bookcase, I read of Pope
Benedict XV, who reconciled dissenting factions within the
Church and denominations without in his encyclical *Ad
Beatissimi*, in which he revived the slogan "Christian is my
name, and Catholic is my family name."[9]

I wondered what was meant by Pius XI, the consummate
librarian and anything but a slouch with the whispered word,
when he silenced Mussolini's "The man is first a citizen" with
"The citizen is first a man."[10]

Who else other than this direct, straight-shooting man
could have unravelled the knotted cords on that "troublesome
old ball of string," the "Roman Question" (the relationship
between the Vatican and the Roman State) to end the Pope's
status as a prisoner of the Vatican and secure Mussolini's
signature on a treaty safeguarding for all time precious traditions
of the Church?

To criticism of his dealings with Mussolini Pius XI did
not answer. Traditionally, popes do not answer because of that
special force telling them who they are — tradition.

Tradition has it that the enormous throne in the tribune
of St. Peter's in Rome encloses the wooden chair thought to
once have belonged to St. Peter.[11]

Tradition has it that the papal altar in the Lateran basilica
contains a table where St. Peter said mass, and where now only
popes may do so.[12]

Tradition has it that in the chapel of St. Lawrence in the
Lateran Palace you will find the twenty-eight marble steps of
the Scala Santa, which was the staircase trodden by Christ in
the house of Pilate.[13]

Tradition has it that the obelisk Caligula brought to

Rome took ninety men and four hundred horses to raise into position. In 1586, when the 320-ton obelisk was moved to its present location, it was saved from crashing when a sailor from Bordighera called out "Water the ropes!" Ever after, the town of Bordighera has had the privilege of bringing palms for Palm Sunday to St. Peter's.[14] That is how traditions are born; something of value alters our perception of time and space and mankind memorializes it repeatedly.

The Sistine Chapel was built to the measurements of Solomon's Temple by Pope Sixtus IV (1471-84) for that reason. There, Michelangelo memorialized Creation and the Last Judgement.

Such treasures as these and the Pieta (the only statue Michelangelo ever signed, because he overheard someone say it must have been done by someone else) are held by the papacy on trust, as covered by the Lateran Treaty of 1929, which stipulates that students and visitors must be able to inspect them as the heritage of all mankind — heritage and sacred treasures of unparallelled quality preserved by tradition, by love, by law.

Mussolini, like countless power-brokers before him, tried to seduce first an immovable Pius XI and next the unflappable Pius XII into accommodating him. But it took the defeat of Mussolini, the humiliation of Italy and the decline of Europe to bring about a noticeable shift in the outlook of the Church.

Pius XII at war's end increased the College of Cardinals to seventy from thirty-eight, with the result that Italian cardinals were at last outnumbered. "This Church," said Pius XII, who could explain himself quite simply when he took on the role of teacher, "does not belong to one race or to one nation, but to all peoples."[15]

I am inclined to agree with those who find the start of our age of terrorism recorded in the *Vatican Journal* of Anne O'Hare McCormick, an American journalist who served as an eye-witness to the papacy through both World Wars.

On July 21, 1943, the allied bombing of the Eternal City shook the whole of the western world. The capital of Christendom under attack stirred the hemispheres. Anne

O'Hare McCormick wrote, "Rome is ancestral to all who share the great heritage of western law and culture."[16]

The studied precision of the bombers shocked and horrified an already demoralized world. McCormick lamented, "The tragedy of Rome where the dividing line cannot be exactly traced between what we want to keep and what we want to smash reflects in a measure the tragedy of our time."[17]

The new age in which this terrorism would reign announced its arrival with a bang not long after; in 1945, on the eve of the Feast of the Transfiguration, science detonated the first atomic bomb.[18]

God had said, "Let there be light." Man had finally answered, "Let there be darkness."

After that unparalleled demonstration of death, the Church had more appeal than ever to frightened modern man. It grew stronger and stood tall on the world stage. Its traditions were honoured. And for its survival, for converts by the million, for its unheard-of clout in even non-Christian countries, the Church bestowed a singular, crowning gift of gratitude. On November 1, 1950, the solemn declaration of the Assumption of the Blessed Virgin into heaven was publicly performed by Pius XII. The Catholic world was all at once united as never before — emotionally, spiritually and intellectually — in celebration of that peculiarity that stood them apart from most other Christian denominations, their devotion to the Mother of God.

Such was the acclaim accorded Mary by Catholics world-wide on this occasion that it momentarily succeeded in flooding the earth with optimism. It was what the world needed, a counterforce to that blinding promise of death that lit up the Nevada desert in 1945. With the declaration of the Assumption of the Virgin, Pius XII reminded all living under the threat of nuclear annihilation of the life hereafter. It was an outstanding demonstration by a gifted teacher in a classroom the size of the world.

For declaring the proclamation of the Assumption of the Virgin to be infallible doctrine, Pius XII joined Pius X as the object of the liberals' wrath. He was excoriated in the smart press by countless trendy philosophers, theologians, historians, critics and reformers, all trying to impress publishers with the variety of ways they could ask "Who does he think he is?"

Hunger for the new transformed the world. An exploding communications media recorded a world in thrall to consumerism. The instant communication of television injected people with all-day doses of one another. Each day the viewer saw the world recreated in his own image by the miracle of television. By 1960 mankind was hooked on itself. Everything, everywhere, was being re-invented daily. Everything, that is, except the Church. The dials were set on change and growth, but the force of Pius XII's person and presence had kept the ingredients simmering on the back-burner all through the '50s.

Protestants, one was given to understand, found him austere, distant, imperious, stern. I did not find him that way at all. Even without the triple tiara, the *sedia gestatoria*, the ostrich-plume fans, the whole Byzantine panoply of pomp and circumstance that accompanied his official appearances, he was an actor who knew how to make an entrance, and the way he delivered his lines you knew he had been studying them for two thousand years.

I was then and am now a rarity, I hear: a happy Catholic, and an eager audience for all the colour, music, art, craft, fiction and non-fiction that is the world studio called the Vatican.

I was not alone in my fascination with him. Movie stars, sports heroes, celebrities of every stripe, creed and discipline flocked to his audiences.

He raised the papacy to a level of popular recognition never before reached. It acquired unprecedented political clout.[19] Catholics in political life predicted the end of the anti-Catholic vote. Hollywood unabashedly undertook the production of a movie called *The Miracle of the Sun*, which dealt factually, tastefully and sympathetically with the characters, events and phenomena of the Fatima story. (I watched it from the middle of a back row of Protestant friends without an iota of reservation.) The papacy was free of scandal. There were no financial problems. One had to refer to the history books to uncover any bad press. Myriad Catholic youth organizations flourished. The large family was not yet a social sin. Even television in those "Leave It To Beaver" years acknowledged that the family reigned supreme. There were not enough Catholic schools to hold the children. The churches were jammed. One might say the last ten years of Pius XII's reign were the high midnight mass of twentieth-century Catholicism.

So stood the state of the Vatican, the papacy and Catholicism on October 9, 1958, when Pius XII died. Who could guess that overnight no amount of tradition, love or law would be able to preserve the greatest treasure of all, the jewel glittering at the heart of Catholicism for nineteen centuries, the most sublime act of communion between the Creator and the created, that sacred intersection of Time and Eternity, the mass, which not only memorializes but re-creates at His very command the life-sacrifice of Redemption by the Son of God.

The new pope, John XXIII, took the world by surprise. World Refugee Year ushered in the '60s. The Poste Vaticane issued a stamp commemorating "The Flight Into Egypt." Did the engraver know something we did not?

3

The Persuaders

It had long been understood that if anyone wanted to destroy Roman Catholicism they would somehow have to get to the heart of the faith, the body and blood of Jesus Christ, its founder, truly real and truly present in that sacrament called "The Blessed." Catholics understood this could never possibly happen. After all, the Blessed Sacrament was protected by the mass. Throughout history people had laid down their lives defending it. It did not matter what the Vatican Council was all about, priests would die on the altar steps rather than allow the mass to be tampered with.

It was, then, with enthusiasm and total confidence that Catholics looked to Rome and the opening of the Second Vatican Council, eighteen hundred and ninety years after St. Peter was crucified upside-down near the spot in the piazza where Caligula's obelisk now stands.

John's aim for Vatican II, we all now know, was to update the Church and reach out to other communions of Christianity. He is on record as having no interest in the Council discussing the tenets of the faith, because, "They are well known and have been sufficiently explained down through the ages." He said, frankly, however, "The truths of the faith are one thing. How they are explained is another."[1] Could he have possibly imagined the excesses such commentary would lead to? "This holy old boy doesn't seem to realize what a hornet's nest he's stirring up,"[2] said Giovanni Battista Montini, the man who would follow John as Pope Paul VI and have to fight the swarm.

As the forces that would dismember Roman Catholicism organized and booked accommodations in Rome, John continued to look for common denominators between the problems of the world and his own. He complained about his curia "I am only the Pope here,"[3] and when asked how many people worked in the Vatican, he replied "About half."[4]

On October 11, 1962, the Second Vatican Council opened. "It's Pentecost," enthusiasts sighed, adding, "all over again," as if they had been at the first one and remembered it favourably.

In the excitement, people could be forgiven for overlooking the fact that between Galilee and Pentecost there first came Gethsemene, then Gabbatha, then Golgotha, and that the first Pentecost took place on a promontory overlooking the ever-burning refuse in the Valley of Gehon, so close one could smell the smoke rising from Gehenna. And of course, everyone forgot that Pentecost was not man-made.

From the very first moment there was the impression given that those bishops, priests and experts who had congregated there were acting as if they were all there was to the Church, as if the hundreds of millions of faithful around the world did not exist.

The first shock waves felt by non-Catholics came from the sight of Catholic bishops currying media favour in endless on-the-spot interviews. "Go forth and teach all nations" had become, in the new age of electronic media communications, "Go forth and be interviewed." The Christian folk hero would no longer be the martyr living and dying for the faith but the individual who got invited back to talk shows.

The first shock wave felt by Catholics was the downgrading of the Latin liturgy and the approval of the vernacular languages in Church prayers and ceremonials. For seventeen centuries, this sacrifice called the mass, this greatest of all crystal moments, like a flash of Creation's first light (become a verb), had been uttered in Latin.

The higher expectations of Christendom dissolved into disorder. A long slide toward confusion followed. For decades, children at the age of reason had the sacrament of confession explained to them. Now the seven-year-old was told instead that he was "a candidate for reconciliation." The words "dialogue," "collegiality" and "charisma" would become so overused, other words could scarcely be heard — words like "sacrament," "grace," "penance."

When John XXIII died in 1963, the world mourned as genuinely as any new orphan. Cardinal Suenens said John made the supernatural seem natural — words curiously appropriate for what was to be the start of a new age of secular humanism.[5]

On the morning of June 17, 1963, the conclave assembled in the Sistine Chapel to elect the new pope. Each of the cardinals was seated on a wooden throne over which hung a silk canopy, in purple for the cardinals created by Pope John, in green for others.[6]

After the cry *"Exeunt Omnes!"* the eighty cardinals were left to the guidance of the Holy Spirit. Libraries are overflowing with published accounts of what occurred in that conclave, about the lobbying, politicking, fears and hopes of those eighty old men. What may be described in future years as the most crucial consistory in the history of the Church was of great interest to the man in the street world-wide. Which way would the ship sail? Would the barque of Peter continue to be navigated by a pilot with two thousand years experience at reading the heavens? Or would it be every man in his own canoe?

Cardinal Montini was chosen, and he elected to be known as Paul VI, due to his earnest desire to be missionary to the modern world. It is said he was recognized from the first as the best-read and best-informed pope of the century. He would also be the first pope to reign in the full glare of modern media.

Whatever else can be said about Paul VI, one thing is indisputable. Central casting would have had to search long and hard to find someone less photogenic. At the very moment when television was defining the standards whereby politicians, athletes, musicians and actors could command trust, be taken seriously, deferred to and granted the benefit of the doubt, a pope emerged from the crucial conclave with a countenance bearing the maximum accumulation of negative image characteristics, the most notable being deep-set, dark-rimmed eyes, a seemingly uncertain glance, an unfortunate propensity for being photographed with his lips parted but shaping no words and a seeming inability to project warmth, mirth or joy. Those times when he was captured in a moment of gladness, alas, an impression of glee seemed to arrest those doleful features.

It was left to the new pope to follow through with the second session of the Second Vatican Council. He would be one of the most betrayed, abused personages in papal history. Those who were thirsty for an overturn of the Church's authority heaped praise on his every innovation while preparing to deny, accuse and ridicule his every attempt to uphold the magisterium.

He continued the work of the Council opened by his predecessor. He seemed, at the beginning at least, oblivious to the fact that the hornet's nest opened up by John XXIII had given wing to a swarm of philosophers and ideologues bent on altering the very shape and purpose of the hive.

John XXIII's straightforward aim for Vatican II had been "to return the Church to the simple form it had when it left the hand of Jesus Christ, its founder." What Paul VI inherited from him was nothing less than a challenge to the very origin, nature and rights of the Church.

It had been three short years since John XXIII, struck by the idea of a council, popped out of bed and threw open the windows of the Church. In that time, philosophers, theologians, critics, historians and reformers flew in looking for ways to free the Church from superfluous ecclesiastical authority, free themselves and philosophy from medieval Christian scholasticism and establish the primacy of human conscience. And they realized they had, as ammunition and reinforcement, something their turn-of-the-century counterparts only dreamed of — a world in love with the idea of liberty, an idea to which popular governments owed their existence and communist regimes, paradoxically, relied for the illusion of popular government. They had both the reality and the myth of democracy at their disposal.

The pot was about to boil over. The recipe for the disaster that was to follow was not new at all but very old. As long ago as 1907, Pius X had recognized it as an aggressive belief system intent on supplanting those sacred truths of which the Church was the depository. Its program for doing so required dismantling the certainties regarding the origin, nature and rights of the Church. The invisible glue holding this usurping force together came from one single directive — to treat as common error the belief that the authority of the Church came from without, from God.[7]

According to this Modernist belief system, the Church has its origin in the individual. Through individual experience, through the natural needs and yearnings of the human heart, the reality of God is discovered. The resulting need to safeguard that discovery and honour it through worship is met when other individuals who have had the same experience group together and a society of individual consciences is formed, in other words, a Church.

Ultimately, of course, this goes against the belief that Jesus Christ instituted the Church and the sacraments. He may be the first believer, according to this argument, the first to have experienced the divine reality through the needs and yearnings of his own heart, but that is that. This not only puts the authority of the Church in question but practically shrugs off the significance of whatever authority Jesus gave to Peter, let alone what it means to his successors, the popes.

The Church, then, is not an institution founded by the actual Son of God but rather it is the joint experience of all those individual consciences who realize the reality of God on their own. This collective possesses its own authority based on the experience of each individual. If the Church denies this and uses its authority without owning up to its responsibility to that collective conscience, then it is tyrannical. The authority of the Church, the rights of the Church, must be subject to the authority of individual consciences. One conscience; one vote.

Clearly, the only way the existing Church can avoid conflicting with individual liberty in this model is to adapt itself to democratic forms. The primacy of the individual conscience must be the hinge on which will swing any conciliation between the authority of the Church and the liberty of believers.[8]

What is more, every believer has the right to work for the common good in the way he thinks best. But the Church, being a collectivity of consciences with its own authority, is also an individual. Naturally, then, since there are belief systems other than ours, they too are individuals and have the right to work for the common good in the way each thinks best. Therefore no Church is better than any other, unless one Church suffers the loss of collectivity of conscience. To prevent our Church slipping in this regard, it is necessary and vital for unity and strength that every rule of discipline, dogma and liturgy must be decided through the non-stop participation of the whole community on the basis of one conscience, one vote.

Pius X had foreseen and worded all of this before the invention of the wireless, automobile, airplane, before television, and seven years before there was a war big enough to be called the First World War. The main weakness of the new belief system was that to challenge the authority of the existing Church, to show how in modern times the existing base of authority of the Church was abusive, tyrannical, and anti-liberty, it needed a focus. In 1907, no one particular focus was strong enough.

Pius X could not have been able to foresee the source of the major challenge to come half a century later. Or maybe he could; the man was a saint and a prophet. At any rate, by the 1960s the ingredients were finally all in place. The focus for the demand for liberty from Church authority was to be birth control and sexuality. By the time the curtain rose on the Second Session of the Second Vatican Council to reveal Paul VI seated in the Chair of Peter, the stage was set for a war to the death between the Church of Christ and "the Church of the People."

How would the salesmen of this new belief system

supplant the old? Simple, they would gradually transform the collective conscience they so insistently proclaimed existed. This would be accomplished by fulfilling their other demand — the reform of the liturgy, which they called "revival." In this they had the Pope's active participation.

Under Paul VI, the Council shaped a vision of the Church supposedly reflecting primitive Christianity in the twentieth-century idiom. Not only was it not intended as an attack on tradition, in some ways an understanding of tradition was actually enhanced. However, the momentum toward change was unstoppable. Paul VI authorized the most complete and fundamental revision of the sacramental rites and the Roman Missal since the Council of Trent. He sanctioned the use of the vernacular, the adoption of regional or traditional custom and the simplification as well as the reform of the liturgy.[9] To the average Catholic, all these alterations were symbolized by two simple changes. The sacrifice of the mass was no longer offered in Latin by a shepherd facing the high altar of Calvary, on behalf of the flock, lovingly protected, at his back. It was said in the language of the community with the priest facing them. But these changes, seemingly simple, were anything but. In reality, the drawbridge had been lowered, the moat had been crossed, the keep had been breached. The mass of the ages was defenceless.

Paul had seemed oblivious to it all. Yet his attitude was recorded in these words: "No one should feel defeated, everyone should be persuaded."[10]

The persuaders were either inept, insensitive, both or worse. The abuse the mass suffered at the hands of the innovators shocked and horrified an already disoriented Church.

In the years following his Council, the number of adults drawn to the faith dwindled, attendance in Catholic schools plummeted, Catholic publications declined or radically altered their venue, or became vanity sheets for the nearest bishop or archbishop.[11] The decline in traditional devotions traumatized the faithful.

Anne O'Hare McCormick's wartime lament never seemed more apt: "The tragedy of Rome where the dividing line cannot be exactly traced between what we want to keep and what we want to smash reflects in a measure the tragedy of our time."

We have climbed slopes with beating hearts many fog-bound early mornings, we Catholics who know the smell of paraffin and charcoal and incense on the soutanes and surplices of our childhood. What a wonderland it was to kneel on those low steps in the early dawn and hear the priest's *confiteor* as the precious stones studding the fabric of the Latin mass made a Sistine Chapel of an altar boy's heart.

Hearing the priest who offered mass comment from the heart on the great mystery he has just offered on behalf of his faithful provided me, as an altar boy, with some of the greatest poetry of my life. A cherished comment delivered long after my altar boy days had faded into the mist of forgotten songs and sonnets occurred in St. Michael's Church in Toronto. A priest known for his accomplishments with the renowned St. Michael's Boys' Choir, delivering his own sentiments from the pulpit, brought me instantly back to the joy of my youth with "The grand Amen is the high Himalayas of the mountain range that is the mass."

Those heaven-touched slopes became the watershed of the pre-conciliar and post-conciliar Church. The mass of the ages was the high ground on which the battle was waged. When the dust settled, the experts had altered the very landscape of the entire battleground between good and evil, heaven and hell, the flesh and the spirit. And it all came down to this: no longer was it the priest who offered mass on behalf of his flock, it was the assembly of believers who would in future offer it together.

The priest turned around to join this community event and the holy order of Melchizedech went straight to the top of the endangered species list. The Holy Sacrifice of Calvary was no more. It was now a banquet of the Table of the Lord. We had turned our back on Golgotha.

How much of it was Paul VI's responsibility?

Peter Hebblethwaite, in his book *In The Vatican* writes that when told by Arrigo Levi, that only in the Soviet Union does the principle of authority remain intact, Paul VI answered,

"Is that a good thing or a bad thing?"[12]

No doubt in every pontificate there comes a moment when the Holy Father looks across the river and recognizes Attila on the opposing bank. In 1963 the pontiff in the midst of the torrent was not Leo the Great; the man who was faced with the sacking of Roman Catholicism was the pope of the doleful countenance, Paul VI.

The gift of his pontificate to the Church would be "that charter of life and love,"[13] as Monsignor Vincent Foy called it, *Humanae Vitae*, the definitive statement on the responsibilities of love. When this sad and silly age is over, mankind will no doubt marvel that this work of compassion came from a Vicar of Christ tormented by the very Church he fathered. Long before the encyclical was delivered to an anxious Church, Paul's adversaries had their agenda in motion.

So much was sacrificed in the name of pluralism that the Church, seemingly overnight, stood stripped of its garments, its beauty, its art, its majestic, eternal music. It is hardly surprising that when Paul VI's *Humanae Vitae* was published in 1968, the words "to be non-sinful every conjugal act must be open to the transmission of life" fell on ears made deaf with uncaring by a decade of mind numbing out-of-tune folk guitars. The theologians who had hijacked the Council now had only to publish that sexual acts and their aftermath were really a matter of individual conscience, and they reaped a tidal wave of popularity.

Paul wondered about it all: "Perhaps the Lord called me to this service not because I have any aptitude for it or so that I can govern and save the Church in its present difficulties but so I can suffer something for the Church so that it will be clear that it is the Lord and not anyone else who guides and saves it."[14]

Paul VI died a broken man. He lay in a plain coffin of cypress wood, set on an oriental rug on the steps of St. Peter's for all the world to see, to praise, to condemn, to shake their heads at; only one Easter candle stood sentinel. On his coffin lay an open Bible, the pages of the Gospel ruffling in the breeze. It was as if Paul were saying, "Say what you may about me, what He says about us is all that matters."

Following on the edicts of Vatican II, provisions were made for experimentation and adaptation of the liturgy. By 1974, however, when the vernacular mass was being actively promulgated, the "liberty of the believer" to introduce innovations and invent ceremony was already something to be guarded zealously by those who shape the Liturgy of the Word and the Liturgy of the Eucharist to their own designs. Both the survival and the obliteration of the mass were possible in 1974.

Hand in hand with the new communal liturgy went the survival or obliteration of the priesthood. And with the priest went the survival or obliteration of the life-giving sacraments which the Modernists had already relegated to the classification of mere "faith-nourishing signs." Along with the sacraments went the survival or obliteration of the hierarchial church, and with it the Kingship of Christ. The goals of the Modernists of Pius X's day had been surpassed beyond their wildest dreams.

In the summer of 1988, Ottawa, Canada's capital, was simmering over the prospect of having unexpectedly dropped into its midst four Oratorian priests and five Brothers whose orthodoxy and conservative style did little to conceal their love for the traditional mass of the ages, the master key to the hierarchial church.

Face to the wind of the Ottawa River with Champlain at my side, as he holds high to the western sky the instrument with which he unravelled the mysteries of this great country, his astrolabe, it is easy to fantasize about some such device that might undo the calamity diminishing the Church today before time makes the damage permanent and the darkness welcome again.

But then, alas, even Champlain's astrolabe was lost, for over two hundred years as I recall.

4

The Dark Ages Were Blinding

The moment I hear one of the current crop of pop theologians refer to the years preceding Vatican II as "the dark ages," I discount him as a reliable interpreter of Vatican II itself. I did not experience "the dark ages" from his lofty vantage point, nor did I live through much of it, but of what I saw I can report quite confidently — it was not so dark! I especially remember the end of that era, for I was of that age when raw emotion makes of the heart a sort of photographic paper on which every sparkle of life is sensitively recorded. Too young and unsophisticated to control the intellectual and spiritual apparatus that determined the amount of exposure one should allow, I was left with imprints filled with sunlight and mystical beams and ghost images.

In the '40s and '50s, being a large Catholic family in the Ottawa Valley meant living out the cycle of the week in response to the calendar events of the church, the steeple of which could be seen just over the trees from our back porch and kitchen window. Feast days, fast days, days of abstinence, all-night fasting before communion, no meat on Friday, the forty hours, daily mass: these dominated our lives and determined its rhythm.

One reason I have always had the greatest respect for the art of theatre management is because I know the value of deadlines, schedules, smooth exits and entrances, movements of large groups of people. That was everyday life in a large Catholic family. Every morning began with a pre-dawn overture of stirring, rumbling, mutterings, squabbles, fights for the washbasin and the mirror, then a sudden swift exit of the noisemakers in response to the last bell from the steeple beyond the trees. The curtain always managed to go up right on time as the attendants raced in the door, hit their pew or dived into their soutanes and surplices. The first act unfolded with precision and built slowly from prayers at the foot of the altar through the *Kyrie* and Collect to the Epistle, Gospel and *Credo*. The second act opened with the offertory, ever building to that great moment of *"Hoc Est Enim Corpus Meum,"* then the great moment of elevation, the mystery of mysteries suspending all minds and hearts: *"Pater Noster, Agnus Dei, Domini non sum dignus."* Then communion, the incomprehensible and incredible made so simple. God for breakfast.

It was a life filled with beauty, colour and silence. I can hear the breeze, even now, that washed over the fields, paths and gardens of that world. For such was the quiet in our pre-television existence up there on the hillside of that little town on the Madawaska River that the cries of a newborn, or the sobbing, bawling and sighing of bickering siblings remain the sounds memory employs to distinguish those days, one from another.

Fences there had only one purpose, to give some shape to the world lived in by the cows that belonged to the convent. They would amble through that rolling, flower-festooned paradise and enhance with their gait and get-lost attitude a rhythm of life that was unmistakably good for the human heart. I never saw a nun milking one of them, but it was in the attempt to catch them at it that my Protestant friend and I slipped through the fence one day.

The Queen Mary was our target. She was a great brown

jersey with an enormous udder that fascinated all of us. She was called Queen Mary because her neck was all white, and my mother said it reminded her of the necklaces the old Queen wore piled up from her collar to her chin. At any rate, it was rumoured that the Queen Mary had not come home the night before, that she must be trapped somewhere, that her bell must have fallen off. The nuns, it was said, had gone out into the fields and trees to look for her, and we naturally assumed they would have to milk her as soon as they found her. So we took off in pursuit, the image of a nun milking a cow drawing us at breakneck speed through fences and over logs.

We came upon the nuns soon enough. Over the top of a dense and roughly grown hedge near the open spaces of the hydro power line we saw a high black prominence bobbing up and down, slowly, pausing at each extreme, then continuing on. Clearly it was the veil of one of the Sisters of St. Joseph pulled tightly over her starched coif. We crept up on them silently, knees and hands slivered with thorns and thistles, until we could count four, five, six, seven nuns all moving in the same purposeful fashion. But there was no Queen Mary in sight. The nuns had aprons pulled over the fronts of their long flowing habits and they carried cans, baskets or pails. They were picking berries.

I lay in the shrubbery alongside my breathless friend and watched them. It seemed to me they looked as much as if they belonged there as they did when they filed into the front-row pews for mass or when they were at the front of the classroom drilling Latin into us by rote. They were a unique and special part of the world we lived in, though their black-and-white habits were supposed to state that they had denied the world; that they had made the commitment to perpetual virginity; that they were married to God. They were detached from the world, yet, oddly, they seemed perfectly at home in it no matter where they were seen. When they strolled the boardwalk on evenings in the summer and spoke softly about secret things, only to one another, they were breathtakingly mystifying. We stayed in the water when they walked by, unprepared to stand on dry ground dressed only in swimming trunks anywhere near such otherworldly creatures. They were a part of my world, yet a world apart. They made it possible to believe that one could live *in* this world and not be *of* it. They were a constant reminder of the existence of God. They were His wives, devoted, beautiful and silent. Perhaps it was the quietness of them that drew me to them the most. Even picking berries, they bobbed up and down like figures in a silent movie, their quietness turning the sounds of nature into clamour and riot.

Who could have guessed that day, as we lay in the brambles and studied them, that they were an endangered species? Who would have believed, had they been told, that they would disappear from the planet under the force of something more mysterious than that which killed the dinosaurs? Who would have guessed that within two decades researchers would have to file through archives and museums to find pictures of what they looked like? Had a child been given to believe then that so much beauty would vanish from the face of the earth, that child would have cried himself to sleep for nights and nights.

Is it not odd how beauty and perfection are always at home in childhood? The Immaculate Conception is accepted matter-of-factly by the seven-year-old, for what could be more sensible than God creating perfect purity?

I well recall the thrill of reading not long ago the new theory that dinosaurs did not disappear at all, that in fact they were still with us, as birds. The theory was a simple one. The dinosaurs lived in the swamps, but the earth grew hot and the swamps dried up, so they started to go inland in search of food. The fastest dinosaurs caught the fast land food and survived. The need for speed prompted them to grow smaller until they could chase food up into the trees. Add one quickly developed breastbone so they could fly and, voilà, birds!

Is it possible, then, that somewhere today there are beautiful, perhaps tiny, flying life forms that once were black-veiled, coiffed in starched linen and layered in multiple floor-length skirts? Did they one day, when they were out picking berries, decide for some reason that it was less anxious up in the trees and make their way up into them? One day, when the world is safe again, will they fly out?

I remember 1959 with such clarity, it is as if my lens had become stuck permanently open. I was seventeen.

Everyone knew "the Fatima Secret" was to be revealed in 1960. It was never known whether the secret would be read aloud at the stroke of midnight or whether another 360-some days of waiting were to be endured before we learned the details. But one thing was certain, Catholic kids got asked to a lot of parties that Christmas, fussed over, traded the best records and phoned constantly on the pretext of getting advice. It was all very systematic. Everyone wanted their own token Catholic as a friend or confidante for what was to come after "Auld Lang Syne."

The story of Fatima had been told in our household many times. It seems I had always been familiar with the details. Three young children in the rocky hills of Portugal are visited by an angel who teaches them to pray. Over the next few months they are visited six times by the Madonna; they witness a miracle in which the sun breaks away from the sky and becomes a wheel of fire. The three seers, the appearance of the Lady of Fatima, the angel who came first, the great miracle of the sun, the incredible array of characters in the village, in the government, in the clergy: it's a story that, once heard in childhood, is never forgotten. It happened to children whose innocence never left them, in a pastoral setting the likes of which adults often dream when the distortions of city life make them old and tired before their time.

There were countless treasures already woven into the fabric of our family life that were inseparable from the main themes of Fatima. The Eucharist, rosary and reparation were what our lives were all about.

I loved the Fatima story always, continued to read about it throughout my life, and even in the years when I did not go to church at all, I could never resist anything and everything printed about it. It remains, for me, the only story ever told that comes close to the story of the first Christmas. A small group of people are compelled to assemble in a particular spot, then required to react to a stupendous happening, in the case of the little group in Bethlehem, nothing less than the Creator of the world taking on the flesh of a child to become one with His creatures. In the case of Fatima, three children, after playing amid their sheep in a pasture with little more to worry them than perhaps wondering what the afternoon would hold, suddenly are made the trustees of nothing less than the future of the world.

Three secrets were confided to the seers. The first two secrets concerning reparation had already been made known. But the third part, written down by Lucia and confided to the Pope through her bishop, was to be made known in 1960, or upon Lucia's death. The belief that it prophesied a calamity for mankind in this century obsessed people for decades.

For 365 days (three and a half centuries in a teenager's time), 1960 dragged on without the Pope saying "May I have the envelope please." Then Christmas was upon us again, and soon another New Year's Eve party.

The last day of 1960 was the most emotional of all my teenage years. To the very last moment of that day, there were those who held out hope that the Secret would come bursting over the radio from the Vatican at the last minute. Surely if our Lady at Fatima had said that the Secret was to be opened in 1960 the Pope would open it. He did not.

The immediate result of the Secret not being broadcast in 1960 was that I had to face up to what the future would become without a cataclysm deciding for me. On leaving grade thirteen in my community in the early '60s, there were really only four worlds to choose from. You were either going to be a nurse, an engineer, a teacher or you were going to work in the mill. That was it. In toto. That there were other choices for teenagers in the world was a rumour we had long heard of, but those who had gone off to find out if it was true never returned, so we had no proof. I chose education.

5

The Deadly Retreat

June 1963. What a year that was to be twenty.

The Peace Corps dominated the soft hearts of young men in those days. The Kennedy years had created the impression that it was possible to get around the globe and do for people less fortunate what you could clearly see needed to be done. The notion that the recipients of such largesse as Canadian teenagers might bring with them should have any ideas of their own about what they wanted did not seem in the remotest way possible. Of course, that attitude was not particular to our generation.

Recently I had the pleasure of visiting in his room in the Manresa Nursing Home in Pickering, Ontario, the colourful old Jesuit Father Roland. He was delighted to get a chance to recall his early days missionizing Native people along the north shore of Lake Superior, and he had his trunkload of memorabilia open before you could say "blackrobe."

He talked a lot about the '30s and '40s and then took out a diary he had kept throughout those years. One page he read aloud will forever remain etched in my memory because it led to a few spoken words that cast a beacon, a light over the mysteries of young men's hearts, that resolved for me many of the doubts I had about my own early years.

The page detailed how Father Roland rode the rails

beneath a boxcar in a sort of metal basket hanging just above the snow and the ties. He would reach such and such a destination, the train would slow and he would roll out onto the railway bank, lie there until the train had finished passing and then go baptize babies, marry some people, bury others, and catch the next convenient train back. Somewhere on that particular day in 1939 when he was travelling from Mount MacKay Mission to Heron Bay he heard a radio report that filled him with joy, and he recorded it thus in his diary.

"Franco takes Madrid. God is on our side!"

I asked him how he could live such a life, how he could keep going year after year in such a bleak pattern, enduring all the hardships and not wishing that he was off in some foreign land representing some vital cause.

He looked at me for a small, silent fraction of time then said in a voice filled with emotion, "We were young. And we were in love."

It was the first time I had ever heard a man say "in love" in that way. The words meant just what they said. A young man falls in love and behaves in all the frightful and dangerous ways in which young men everywhere behave when they have fallen head over heels in love with a girl. But in this case, the young man fell in love with God.

That moment in a quiet nursing home, alongside a trunk full of memorabilia, was of inestimable value to me. Something calmed down within, some anxiety, some worry, some concern about my emotions and the direction in which my heart had been advancing and retreating for years. That moment has helped me through this last decade, when my fears for the Church I grew up loving were multiplying at an awesome rate.

Back there in 1963, with only weeks remaining of the worst educational experience a human being can go through — teachers' college — I was invited to attend a weekend retreat held by an Oblate in a house in the centre of the city. To this day I wish I had never gone.

But then, having been raised on stories of people being called by God and what happens if you do not bother to answer, I thought, maybe a weekend is not much to give up to keep on the right side of the ledger. So I went.

Convincing myself that being locked inside a house with a dozen other young men for three days would be very much like a Peace Corps adventure, I arrived, was booked in, took stock of the other faces I saw and acknowledged, sinkingly, that none of them were in the least bit adventuresome. I immediately took to my room to measure the enormity of my error in coming.

What happened at the first session I cannot recall, except that before it had ended, I had selected three faces that I was certain would end up going into the seminary. They all looked to me like men who would go bald, lose all their colour and smile a lot. That was what I had imagined to be the fate of anyone who left that retreat with an invitation to join the Oblates.

I forgot everything discussed, fought the intense claustrophobia by sparring with my fantasies, which came and ravaged me without end and without mercy, and awaited the last meeting, Sunday evening, with something near to wild abandon. I had escaped being categorized, cornered, convinced that I should join the others and become a seminarian. We convened, shook hands and everyone left. Except me. The room emptied while I stood looking, dumbfounded, at the retreat director. Of the twelve or fourteen men who had arrived there on Friday, I was the only one invited to consider going to the seminary in Winnipeg.

To say I was surprised and horrified does not come close to the truth. I think for a few short moments all the blood in my body fled to some remote corner of my being whence it refused to return, for I could neither think, feel, taste nor prove that any other of those senses that I had come to rely upon as a hot-blooded young man of twenty would ever be functional again.

The month that followed was lived in a state of terror. Had I an appointment with the hangman I could not have felt any more certain that it was all about to end — my life as I knew and liked it. I made preparations, got my parents' agreement, then began to look around and tally all the things I would be missing in the world out there beyond the seminary walls. All this because I could never have imagined laughing it off. What if the retreat director was truly a man of God and right? Could

I, raised a Catholic, laugh off what might have been" the call"?

By graduation I had a frighteningly long list of things I would miss.

I left the graduation dance and asked the priest chaperoning the event to take me for a drive. In the car I told him I could not do it. Could not go. That it felt more like death to me than anything to do with life as I had been living it. Of course that was exactly the case, and exactly his point, but he was kind and tried his best to relate to me by interpreting hit songs coming over his car radio in the light of our conversation.

When "I Will Follow Him" came on the air, I knew I could not escape whatever lesson he would draw from that, so I told one of the biggest lies of my life.

"I can't go because my parents need me."

That lie has haunted me to this day. Its guilty shadow has re-emerged repeatedly, very often when I am alone, in hotel rooms, selling a typewriter or packing for yet another move to yet another smaller and cheaper apartment. My hair is gone. I occasionally catch glimpses of a colourless man accompanying me in store windows and bank windows and recognize the nightmare I had back in the retreat house in 1963.

Yet the lie served to free me. So relieved was I to escape the seminary that I went out and misbehaved splendidly for two and a half days with my Protestant friend, who welcomed me back to the world with righteous glee. He had remained suspicious of all things Catholic since that last day of 1960 when the Secret had not been opened. From that day on, his response to anything Roman was accompanied by an emphatic, "Oh, yeah? Show me!" attitude.

How could I show him? It took thirty years for people to realize 1960 was the beginning of the end of the Catholic Church as we knew it, that within three decades a revolution from within would have accomplished what the Reformation, the French Revolution and communism could not — the emasculating of the Roman Catholic Church, a usurpation of her power, an upending of her priorities that would result in a near total subjugation of the magisterium to the "authority" of the people.

How could I show him that in thirty years the Catholic Church would lie spoiled and dismembered, landfill for those futurists who crave an environment without the Incarnation.

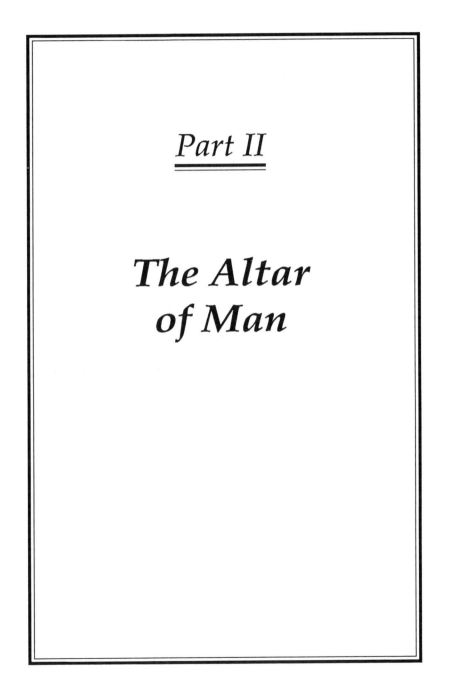

Part II

The Altar of Man

1

Bonfires

"I long for the gardens of Córdoba."

When the incomparable Alec Guinness spoke those words as King Faisal in *Lawrence of Arabia*, he had just finished marvelling at how the British were fascinated by the desert. This he found odd. "There is nothing in the desert," he said.

His longing for Córdoba was not mere nostalgia. It was a yearning for the stature that had once been Islam's. A yearning for the muscle of its creed. And yes, what would be more natural for a desert king than a yearning for the fountains, the sparkling mystery of the air, sun and sky of Andalusia as seen through beading water. A yearning for the fullness of life, for him, the fullness of faith, truth, goodness and beauty.

Since long before the psalmist wrote it, man has known where to go to find all of that – "I will go unto the altar of God, to God the joy of my youth."

Alas, today, within the Roman Catholic Church, the altar of God has been usurped. There now stands in its place the altar of man. It has taken man a mere thirty years to banish God from the garden. And without Him it is withering to the root.

When those three great fountains of adoration — Psalm 42, Psalm 25 and John 1:1-14 — were struck from the Immemorial Mass, the garden of God was denuded of its lush entrance, cascading water, mountains of light. The mass of the ages was reduced to a minimalist landscape, stark and mean. The brook for the yearning deer ceased to run. The bread of heaven once more came to a desert that was bleak and sub-bleak. I marvel that anyone could prefer it to the orchard that once stood there. But, of course, there are those who do, and they spend an astonishing amount of energy in the Church today, all in the name of a new age shaped by and for man. They are making sure that the Church will never return to what it once was.

In the late '50s an antique buyer searching rural Quebec for Canadiana was directed to a certain farm to see furniture "of great value." He located the farm just in time to see an outdoor bonfire consume a small mountain of hand-carved oak, ash and maple furniture. When asked his reason for being at their gate, the distraught buyer told the owners he had come to see their furniture "of great value." At once the owners opened the gate and ushered him into the kitchen, where they proudly displayed for the visitor their new chrome table and chairs.

In the mid-80s, parishioners arriving for Friday morning mass at a venerable old church in Toronto found the doors inexplicably locked. They remained locked for all that day and the day after. When they approached the church for Sunday morning mass, they found the church's once-beautiful high altar in slivers on the asphalt of the parking lot. The church doors, however, were now open. Rushing inside, they found the sanctuary denuded of all evidence of the externals of the life-giving sacraments, and in their place were a table for an altar and a felt banner saying "Rejoice."

Such absurdities as these are common fare to Catholics who have watched with sorrow for three decades now as iconoclasts, in their desperate drive to rid the present of any debt to the past, rip, splinter, burn and deface all reminders of who we are and how we got that way.

We are much in need of such reminders right now, we Roman Catholics, for it is from our very own ranks that the greatest threat to the cultural patrimony of the Church has emerged. Did I say emerged? It exploded into existence! A veritable reign of terror has been waged without abating for thirty years now. In the front ranks, destroying sacred art, music and architecture, are none other than priests, nuns and laity, the new iconoclasts, conducting a ruthless, wilful campaign against artistic freedom and excellence.

The farmer in the Gaspé burns the evidence of an impoverished past. The Modernist cleric, returning from a seminar on syncretism, throws out the high altar that once proclaimed he was unique, a gifted soul tending camp, oiling the lamps so others could find their way to the Field of the Kingship of Christ. In his wake, the great cathedrals of Western civilization have been replaced by Glory and Praise Handshake Boutiques.

In my need to comprehend how the Church, the single greatest patron of the arts throughout history, could have allowed itself to become subject to guerilla tactics, I plagued heritage architects, conservators and historians with appeals. None of them could clarify the tragedy of our lost patrimony with greater simplicity and eloquence than the late Father Donald Neilson, whose one-word answer cut like a knife through the Gordian knot of Modernist pretension now tyrannizing the Catholic Church. I came upon him one day as I was studying the interior of the Oratory.

"Shadows," he said, when I asked him what was the single most important thing architects need to understand about Catholicism.

Having once directed the planning and building of a church of his own, he described the battle he underwent to ensure that the interior would include pillars to provide shaded areas. He explained his belief that the Catholic who has been away a long time returns to the shadows and gradually, as he re-establishes his relationship with God, makes his own way into the light, man-made light that represents the True Light. All creation now and then needs shade and shelter from the sun and from the face of God.

Yes, I thought, for God is brighter than the sun and has no shadow.

Did Michelangelo know that? Did he paint God a

shadow?

No one wants to paint like Michelangelo any more. After all, those pictures of God and saints and martyrs that used to fill churches — were they not an invention of the Middle Ages, to teach people who could not read? And those vestments were invented for people who needed feudal lords, and those ceremonies were for, well, to instill order, you know. There's a religion course on that at school. People don't pay attention to that sort of thing any more.

Some used to get away with it, back in the days when we were simple-minded and could be cowed with talk about Original Sin and the First Fall. But no more, not since our Original Goodness was unearthed by theologians digging for proof that God was a woman.

How they used to carry on, those early Catholics! All that ceremony about God being something "up there."

All that is gone now. It was jealousy that did it in. Human jealousy of God. All that "exquisite detail," it smacked of privilege. And anyway, the brilliance was blinding.

Sameness was the solution, the goal of the uninspired, serving a fantasy of equality. So they took paint rollers to the open tomb and bathed it in grey, the colour of shadow.

And the Sistine Chapel, reflected onto the walls of each altar boy's heart by the precious stones studding the fabric of the Latin mass, became just a single-line cartoon.

Paul VI travelled the globe in his zeal to imitate his namesake, St. Paul, the apostle to the Gentiles. But his tenure will be remembered most for the impression left on the faithful. By the end of Paul's pontificate, the mass, which had been the glory of the ages, now, to some, had become a parody of a television family sitcom, with Dad presiding at table amidst a meagre brood of altar attendants, the number reflecting responsible planned parenthood. This "presider" then filled his twenty-eight-minute time slot with smoothly delivered one-liners while being interrupted at regular intervals by lay salespersons marketing scripture to promote such causes as women on the altar and absolutely anything and everything happening in Latin America.

Sin had become as outdated as black-and-white movies.

Consciences had to be colorized, pluralized, neutralized, urged writers of the new order.

The art of churches was thrown out or painted over, sacred vessels went to flea markets, church architecture was vandalized for the sake of "contemporizing."

The sanctuary became a seminar room designed by theologians accustomed to being applauded in class.

Uphill from the Oratory, near the University of Ottawa, stands a church that is the result of trying "to return the Church to the simple form it had when it left the hand of Jesus Christ, its founder." It is named after St. Joseph; what a shame that the great carpenter from Nazareth should be commemorated in a building where evidence of Roman Catholicism has been hopelessly lost.

Reputed to have once rivalled Notre Dame for the quality of its furnishings, architecture and art, St. Joseph's now stands barren, lifeless, colourless, like a great, gutted whale beached on ever-shifting post-conciliar sands. It is a church run by the Oblates of Mary Immaculate, once the inexhaustable, uncompromising hand-servants, as their title professes, of the Mother of God.

One suspects immediately upon entering the semi-gloom of this church that it is one of those "spaces" run by individuals for whom Vatican II is an addiction. You know who they are — every parish has them. Most parish councils are controlled by them. They are committee junkies, fellowship freaks. Their entire post-1965 vocabulary serves one purpose — to somehow lever the word "collegiality" into each speech, address, homily, sentence, phrase and utterance. They mainline on the so-called "Spirit of Vatican II," requiring weekly doses of improvisation to sustain their "compassion" for their "community of believers" and "neighbours in liturgy."

These people, if given the choice, would no doubt chart a new calendar dating all history as BVII or AVII. They are singularly incapable of dealing with or facing up to anything that happened or existed or was thought of before Vatican II. Such parishes are invariably dominated by Modernists who look back at 1960 the way Wile E. Coyote looks over a cliff.

St. Joseph's is the perfect example of what happens if ill-informed but highly opinionated parishioners are allowed to reinterpret church interiors. A treasury of the sacred, built up over centuries, can vanish without a trace. If the priest is a push-over, the church interior will become a war zone of homespun ideas fighting for attention. Suddenly, individuals who could not qualify for a job rearranging furniture in a Brownie pack bunkhouse have *carte blanche* to decorate or re-do a sanctuary. The results can be an appalling display of ignorance and arrogance.

On the floor of this sanctuary, just feet from the table altar, is an eight-foot, kidney-shaped goldfish pond, made of three rows of stacked bricks and floored with green plastic garbage bags. Goldfish flash through the murky water.

The one-hundred-year-old oak confessionals are now coat closets complete with hangers. Above the table altar hangs a flat surface, shaped like a movie screen, with some child's smear of colours roughly representing a "V" shape.

Invariably, in cases like these, smears blamed on children turn out to be the maximum artistic output of some liberated nun or teacher who found herself alone in the art supply room for an hour. If the "child art" mounted in sanctuaries, to the stupefaction of the faithful, were suddenly accredited some sort of precious, priceless, primitive art status by a *New York Times* art critic some Groundhog Day, a stampede to Manhattan would empty convents all over North America by Valentine's.

To the left stands a piano, and directly above it on a platform a bank of stacking chairs, teetering in the direction of the table altar. In short, a sacred interior has been turned into a Romper Room, where, clearly, what with ribbons hanging from the sanctuary ceiling and banners slung here and there, Girl Guide show-and-tell is the order of the day. This isn't worship. This is day-care.

That no sense of the sacred survives in this abused interior prompts one to wonder what could possibly become of ceremony here. Not even past exposure to the absurd excesses the laity has brought to sanctuaries would prepare you for the answer found in this setting.

Michael MacEachern, co-founder of *The Orator*, an

Ottawa publication advocating a return to sanity by nuns, priests, bishops and the laity, uses these words in reporting on a "People Church" event celebrating environmental responsibility:

> Vestal virgins wafted down the aisle and cavorted in the sanctuary while alternately worshipping pieces of ribbon, a giant earth ball, a dead tree, and one another. The earth ball was tossed from one end of the church to the other so all present could touch the earth with tenderness, touch the earth with love. Nailed to what was once the high altar was a huge sun. This sun-God device also received due reverence and worship while Christ sat alone in His tabernacle, unnoticed, not even a vigil light to acknowledge His presence.[1]

Be reminded that we are talking here about Catholicism in the capital city of Canada.

Although it was not in evidence this day in St. Joseph's, there was at one time a layer of sand on the floor, presumably so parishioners could experience "Footprints in the Sand"!

This extravagant lunacy can be blamed on kindergarten supervisors gone mad with sudden parish council power, but really the blame lies squarely on the priests who allow it, who will do anything, permit anything, encourage anything as long as it makes them appear *au courant*, as long as it keeps a militant nun or glowering chairperson from writing to the bishop. They know only too well that the last thing they can expect if their parish councils turn on them is support from their bishop.

How did this come about? By what method was the emasculation of the priesthood accomplished? How did the priest become as flexible, pliable, one-dimensional as a male soap opera lead? Programming. The most accessible kind of programming.

2

Test Pattern

The devaluation of the mass that was already underway in 1963 and had reached endtime proportions by 1967 occurred without my notice. Those years flashed by in a blur. Being Catholic was one of my lesser concerns. I do remember Bishop Jennings returning from the Council and having a press conference in the auditorium of the teachers' college. It was jammed with people of every creed. Interest in the Council was genuine, and it was important, if one wanted to be "in," to keep up on the details.

The good bishop lost an opportunity to do great things for ecumenism that night. Not because he did not have the facts, not because he did not have an eager audience, but because his powers as an orator were just slightly less than what God gave radishes. The most important event of the year was the dullest two hours ever spent squirming between other squirmers in the back of the standing-room-only hall.

After that, I remember going to mass in Winnipeg, Vancouver, Toronto, and not noticing much. Then I ended up in Montreal for Expo 67 and saw my first mass in the round.

I remember it because that day I had gone to mass to be close to God. I needed Him, was disoriented by life and lost loves and, well, just needed Him. I did not need, however, to stare across a table altar at a hundred faces staring back at me, in raked seats that gave them the appearance of being at a bullfight, all searching the arena to see who might play the bull to my reluctant matador.

I suspect it was a sudden and swift erosion of confidence that caused the Church to change overnight. What happened to the priesthood I can understand to a degree. All of their lives, they had represented authority that came directly from Christ, through the apostles and the Church. Love them or hate them, they were the centre of whatever whirlwind in which you found them, determined to intervene on behalf of God in the affairs of men. Reject them, slander them, despise them or suffocate them with sentimental attentions, they were expected to survive, for theirs was an authority totally independent of the ways of the world.

Then, alas, those who would be movers and shakers in the Church, who could not be so under the present structure because they had no claim on its authority, put the wheels in motion to turn the Church upside-down. Authority would in future come from the bottom, from the people. The democratization of the Church would destroy the priesthood. Priests were now totally at the mercy of those same minds who had recently discovered that re-ordering sanctuary furniture, rewriting the liturgy and dictating the terms under which the priest would appear at the altar was much more fun than convening bake sales. The priest became the guest of honour at his own humiliation. He was allowed to leave his chair and approach the altar only after every self-obsessed convenor in the parish had a chance to perform.

It had all started with the *Ed Sullivan Show*. Catholics stayed home in droves to watch it, and sooner than you could say "Vespers," benediction was cancelled. Television aerials sprouted atop church rectories. The final seduction of the priesthood had begun. Then every convent got a television, and the nuns learned all about the Third World.

Priests stayed home, got off their feet and watched hour after hour of Hollywood's happy endings. Good times replaced good news. Soon new altars were installed; they looked like TV trays. All that black-and-white television was, of course, really grey on grey. All the church interiors were painted grey and the statuary spray-painted so that St. Teresa soon looked an awful lot like Loretta Young.

The TV aerial became a prophetic parody of the fate in store for the cross above the altar. Satellites ended the need for aerials; crosses were thrown out of sanctuaries and replaced by the floating resurrection apparatus which, without the cross, said no more or no less about the faith than the peacock did about NBC.

About the same time that priests stopped going to retreats and started holidaying in the Caribbean, they slowly began substituting a suit and tie for the Roman collar. Curiously, far from individualizing them, it just made them all look more alike, and all exactly like Robert Young on, you guessed it, "Father Knows Best." Soon after their second or third holiday in Aruba or Cancun, their sanctuaries started looking suspiciously like lobbies in the Ramada Inn, empty, except for a few cushy chairs and a lot of durable carpet.

The talk show inspired endless gymnasium conferences with nuns and priests trotting out their best witticisms about sex education and marriage counselling. Confessionals became sound booths, like they had on "The $64,000 Question." No longer were the innermost secrets of the soul to be whispered in careful darkness to a forgiving Christ, they were to be discussed in the way you discuss your credibility when applying for credit or a new bank loan — applying for an extension on God's patience.

To counter these new influences, the priest relied on what he knew of his audience. They would stick with him as long as he could convince them not to change channels. He became a smiling talk-show host, eternally chatty, eternally friendly. Where the talk-show host greeted everyone with a meaningless kiss, the modern priest used the handshake, equally meaningless, promenading down the aisle to grab hands and look his contestants in the eye while above the TV-tray altar where the cross used to be hung a screen, like the gameboards on TV, where trendy hymns could be flashed for all to sing along.

The effect of the first television decade on the priesthood was just a test pattern for the big show that was to follow.

Years have passed. Now the priest sits centre sanctuary where once the holy tabernacle stood, grinning grotesquely as every abuse imaginable is perpetrated within arm's reach.

If priests could cave in under such pressure now, I often wonder, what would they have chosen as options had they been confronted by the sans-culottes?

3

Caterpillars

If priests had a sudden and tremendous sense of loss to deal with, it was hardly surprising; after all, they'd lost nothing less than the guardianship of that authority for which they had given up the world.

Nuns, on the other hand, and their reaction to the pressures of the first Vatican II decade, present no such clear picture to the bewildered Catholic who grew up loving them for their visibility as non-conformists.

The sisters fell prey to "performance." They heard the phrase "role-play" and fell for the old "in the round" nonsense that had come out of experimental live theatre in the early '60s.

"Role-playing" was a phrase one heard endlessly in 1967. When children were brats, they were only "role-playing." When teenagers shot up a liquor store they were "acting out." When teachers wanted to sow enthusiasm among their federation members, they would throw a convention where all would role-play a line of picketers striking for more pay six years before they got the right to strike. It was all the legacy of the first television generation. Everything was performance. The most unlikely people fell in thrall to it.

I have always believed that without the wholesale exodus from sanity of the nuns of the Catholic Church, the mass would still, today, be the object of that reverence that preserved it for centuries.

Women's issues were all the rage, and in no time the good sisters had lifted themselves out of the shadows where a celibate male clergy had kept them and separated into a new species. Overnight they cast off their elegant, mysterious costumes and adopted homely little uniforms that made them look just slightly less interesting than check-out clerks at Canadian Tire.

Now you could not tell them apart from real estate agents. Now they could compete with men for those Church jobs. They were everywhere.

They left the cloister and hit the sanctuary running, feverishly determined to deal with issues of interest to them. Liturgies were improvised to allow the Sisters the chance to do a lot of role-playing in the round, experimenting endlessly on how best to harness the charismatic.

These experiments in liturgy began as a means of drawing people together on social issues and quickly devolved into a forum for the needs that obsessed the Sisterhood — women in the church, women on the altar, women and sexuality, women priests.

It was an experiment, like young people's theatre of the '60s all over again. However there was a major difference; that was church theatre. This was theatre church.

By the end of the 60s, teaching within the Separate School system, I was surrounded daily by evidence of the changes of the lives of the religious.

Sister Burt was the first nun I ever knew whom I would describe as being totally corrupted by role-playing in the round. One day she was in the habit of the Sisters of St. Joseph, the next she was in a sad little black-and-white waitress uniform with veil. One week after that, in what I remember as nothing more than a flash in time, she was in a tidy little blue suit and blue beanie, with matching blue overcoat, much like the formula-stitched, sculpted suits of armour that the Queen wears. She appeared at my classroom door in this outfit; the butterfly had become a caterpillar. A friend who was visiting remarked afterward that the lady in blue smiled like Burt Lancaster, and so she did.

Sister Burt was ripe for role-playing in the round. She was about thirty-five and almost certainly a virgin (as well she should have been). She was frightening to have a conversation with. So unaccustomed was this woman to dealing with human beings while not in her veil and long skirt that she seemed almost manic. It was tremendously disconcerting to realize, after puzzling for an hour over her strange behaviour, that her speech, eye movements and gestures were anything but demure.

"Don't you know?" said my friend Allie when I asked what Sister Burt had been up to.

"No, I haven't the faintest."

"She was flirting with you!" said Allie matter-of-factly.

Immediately upon her saying so I knew it to be true. I had not realized it — who would have expected it coming from a nun?

"That's incredible," I said.

"Don't feel so flattered," said Allie. "She was flirting with me, too."

And that, unfortunately, was the case. Sister Burt was the perfect example of a nun so disoriented by suddenly being thrust into the world on the same footing as the creatures she once prayed for that she did not know how to act at all. In fact, she did not even know she was flirting. She was just one of the long line of the unveiled who tried picking up from where they left off when they entered the convent, to the utter dismay of the Catholics around them, who had to watch grown women go through all the passions and puppy loves usually burned out of teenagers by the time they are fourteen. There is nothing in the world more embarrassing than having to watch a grown adult learn the difference between coy and vulgar.

Unabashed flirting flourished all through the late '60s between the unveiled and the sinful masses, not to mention with some of the silliest men God ever gave lips to — those priests who flashed around town in suits and ties and rings on their fingers and Club Med tans.

In no time at all, the real estate agent was running off with the talk-show host. They did not leave the Church. Far from it. As any good agent knows, the three most important things in real estate are location, location, location. They came back as a team and took over religious education in the separate schools!

Sister Burt married her talk-show host. They had four children. I would like to be a fly on the wall when one of the little grinners asks, "What did you do before you were married, Mommy?"

"I was a bride of Christ," she will answer.

"If you were married to Christ how come you could marry Daddy?"

"Well you see, he was sort of married to Christ too."

"Oh, like Christ came between you."

"Sort of, dear, yes."

"So what did you do, dump him?"

Of all the dreary analogies repeated *ad infinitum* by members of the misty-eyed Vatican II fan club, none grated more than one comment of Sister Burt's. One day, as the staff was discussing the speed with which the Church was collapsing into chaos all around, she assumed a simpering smile and glanced around wistfully.

"The Council," she sighed, "is like a pebble dropped into a pond. It will send ripples of change over the surface of the world until the end of time."

Then, as now, I disagreed with her optimism. If anything, the Council was like a boulder striking the windshield, fragmenting the glass into infinite separations, cracks, shards, slivers — shattering the supposedly shatterproof surface into a million mini-shatters.

Sorrow is the only word to describe the feeling Sister Burt left with me. That the Church I love should have been represented by that silly woman causes more pain than I care to detail. By her words and actions she cast a shadow over all the sainted women in veils who preceded her for centuries. In the process, she managed to steal part of my innocence.

Once, however, that same year, an ancient nun arrived at

the school from Scotland. She had lived in a cloistered convent all her life and was now in her seventies. When the old lady arrived and paid a visit to the staff room, she dismantled forever all the pretensions and precocity of horrid Sister Burt by the simple elegance of her appearance and her manner. She still wore the magnificent habit of the Sisters of St. Joseph, high starched coif, bib, long black skirts with rosary at the belt and a long flowing veil. To add to the startling drama her appearance made, she was almost doubled over at the waist with curvature of the spine. To talk to people, she angled her head in a special way so that, her veil falling on the opposite side and almost touching the floor, she could converse without it hindering her vision.

Until that utterly wonderful old creature visited that day, I had not realized that my response to a disintegrating Church was to drop away. Now here it was looking me in the face, ancient, worn, bent and broken, needing an arm to lean on, needing help, yet totally capable of imprinting on souls the truth about life — that it is interrupted by death but is destined to go on forever.

4

About Those Lay Ministers

The mania for committees and councils now possessing the Church is the natural product of the social worker mentality unleashed and running amok within the institution. The result is an elaborate network of therapy groups for adult runaways addicted to self-esteem. But they are not called "groups," "programs" or "projects," they are called "ministries."

The Eucharistic Ministry

Of those responsible for the loss of beauty in the Church since Vatican II, no one is more culpable than the Church's lay ministers. The mindless behaviour of this superficially trained laity brings to the sanctuary a pomposity that is both embarrassing and saddening to watch. Every parish seems to have at least one self-impressed, puffed-up, strident lay person who behaves as if, just now on the way to church, he single-handedly parted the Red Sea and therefore considers the sanctuary an anti-climax. Their complete lack of a sense of the sacred robs the altar of God of its sacred rights. Eucharistic ministers are the worst of the lot. In the past altar boys wore gloves to handle the sacred vessels, then suddenly women and men in sweatsuits were thrusting their hands into tabernacles and handing out bowls of hosts with no more sense of purpose than a fast-food caterer.

The sense of the sacred is gone. How is a child to revere the communion host when upon his arrival in the vestibule at church a basket of hosts, uncovered, is found sitting atop a rickety ten-by-ten-inch table for all the world to pick at, play with, pocket or poke? How is the Real Presence in the tabernacle to be contemplated if lay ministers refuse to acknowledge that it differs in any way from the breadbox on the counter at home?

Each church seems to have its assortment of lay persons who approach the tabernacle with key in hand as if they were going to the fridge for a beer, making it quite clear to everyone watching that they consider genuflecting or bowing a most grievous imposition on their new status. They seem to take particular pleasure in rooting around in there (once they have thrown it open) as if it might contain the lost keychain that has caused them so much inconvenience all week.

Do the women who refuse to show reverence toward the sacred vessels while serving as lay ministers think they are advancing the cause of women on the altar by rejecting any and all time-honoured courtesies by the priest to the Body and Blood of Christ?

The beauty of gracious human conduct is gone.

The Music Ministry

"The patron saint of mediocrity" the inconsolable Salieri called himself in *Amadeus*. In writing that marvellous phrase, playwright Peter Shaffer comforted everyone who had endured what the Singing Nun and "Domenique-nique-nique" did to the music of the Catholic Church.

Somewhere along the way, someone told the Sisterhood that you could at one stroke punish an entire church of sinners if only you learned one chord on the guitar. Soon after, stout little nuns strapped to five-string guitars were seen in choirs all over North America. "Cumbaya" was done to death in the

'70s by those nuns who had thrilled to it endlessly at Girl Guide camp back in the '50s. Then other nuns found the twanging of that guitar absolutely irresistible. Strumming seemed to have endless attractions for the nuns in the choir loft in the early '70s. The inevitable, of course, happened. Sisters Stout and Twang realized that not only could they completely dominate the auditory facilities of all those sinners down there below, but they could seize hold of their sight as well if they just moved their little show down to the altar. So the campfire girls took up their stance alongside the readers' podium where the number of variations on one chord was demonstrated with unstinting determination well into the '80s.

The sing-along was not far away, complete with pitch-pipe, reducing parishioners who had grown up on sublime and soul-riveting Gregorian Chant to kindergarten-level idlers who had to be entertained whether they wanted to be or not.

I will not go on here about the levels of mediocrity perpetrated wherever the liturgy is geared, supposedly for the satisfaction of children, to the demands of a mediocre guitarist. The assumption operating here is that adults will endure it because guitar sounds supposedly make hymns more accessible to children. The truth is, children saturated with television are the better critics, can spot a mediocre guitar-strummer by the end of the first chord and are bored senseless by the saccharine singsongs they accompany.

The tape recorder was also in use by the '80s and it too began in the choir loft. A great clunk would be heard as the on-switch was turned, then the favourite songs some woman from last week's strawberry social just taped in her very own basement would pitch forward from a rasping speaker and shower the congregation below with non-musical static.

But the tape recorder was not long up there in the choir loft. No, you see, that meant someone had to stay up there to ka-thunk it off and on. One auspicious day, the tape recorder, a large old reel-to-reel contraption, was arranged rather cieverly as a doorstop at the back of the church under the choir loft, so that the priest, upon making his entrance in vestments and smile, could, with one deft swing of the foot, kick it into "play." Now the avalanche of static that had dropped from the choir loft could actually roll after him up the aisle until he turned to face the people.

Music, I was told by a sympathetic and wise priest, is intended to worship God. Tape recorders cannot worship God. Alas, it is to the sorrow of the Church I love that priests have put into the hands of the strawberry-social set the sacred rituals that centuries of love and thousands of elevated souls have shaped. What was once man's very best effort at showing gratitude to the Divine has become a hideous embarrassment.

There was a time when a stir would pass through the church when a non-Catholic walked in. You sat watching them all through mass, knowing that time and again non-Catholics had been moved by the soaring masses of Palestrina and Bach, and you wanted to share the moment with them, so that when they glanced around and sighed with appreciation you could say "See?" as if somehow being Catholic and having great music were inseparable realities. Now one lives in terror that a stranger might come in and actually see what is going on.

The Ecclesiastical Design Ministry

"People Church" architecture is responsible for those brick monstrosities thrown up all over the continent, the churches built since Vatican II.

Blights on the landscape within a decade of their erection, trendy and therefore out of date instantly, they look for most part like firehalls when the trucks are out. Within these ego-bunkers no concession is made to God either in architecture or art. It is "I will not serve" architecture. Great expanses of uninterrupted brick might be broken by a pane of opaque glass, hovering lifelessly above a sloping theatre floor, a homely table altar and, of course, the empty chair, sitting front and centre. It is the tyranny of the mediocre and its fruit, an eternally lamentable example of mean-spiritedness that denies the eye its natural craving for focus, form, shape.

The lesson begins with what Modernist France has done with the French Revolution. All the *Liberté, Egalité, Fraternité*, shouted about on Bastille Day in the Paris of the 1980s, two hundred years after the Revolution, took place without the shadow of a guillotine falling on any cobblestones anywhere. To hear them tell it, the guillotine never existed. The Champs Elysées became a playground and everyone sang songs of Liberty as if they had invented it and given birth to themselves.

In their celebrations they have eliminated the thing that symbolized what changed them. And that's the whole point of the Modernist manipulation of the mass — to eliminate that thing that changes us. What the Modernists have achieved in the Church is to reduce the Passion to a Bastille Day celebration. The aisle has become a playground and everyone sings infantile rhymes about freedom as if they had invented it and given birth to God. And the cross is nowhere in sight. The shadow of the cross falls on no one. Because that way Calvary never existed.

That is why the Church is not Catholic any more — because Catholics go all the way.

Even in grade school, I could never understand why some people favoured the painting of the Last Supper over all other religious art. It was not because of the eucharist. It was, I am sure, because it looked like a party. If the whole drama had only ended there, well then, no one would have to endure the discomfort of meditating on Gethsemane and the Via Dolorosa and Calvary.

We (the Catholics who fell victim to the Modernists) retreated from Calvary long ago — out went the crosses. We retreated from the Via Dolorosa — out went the Stations. We retreated from Gethsemane — out went confession and self-examination. In came social work. Group therapy. Ministries.

It is only a matter of time before Jesus is recognized as the original social worker; then "People Church University" can award Him an honorary degree posthumously. And — at last — they will have Him where they want Him!

A quick scan of the interior of the Modernist Church always leaves one question lingering in mid-air: Who is that "presider's chair" waiting for? How did a term so alien to the language of the Kingship of Christ manage to usurp the space formerly assigned to the externals of that Kingship? Who is the anticipated usurper? No one really believes for a moment that this "presider's chair" business has anything to do with the form and furnishings of primitive Christianity. You might get a few glad-eyed ex-nuns of "People Church" to put aside their political finger-painting long enough to acknowledge they believe that, but let us face one reality: of all the manner and means employed by the Modernists to perpetuate their grip on the Church, none is more transparent than their compulsion to re-invent the universe every morning. Symbols, not specifically the "People Church" symbols, are the signature of revolution wherever it occurs. The Tribune of Paris knew that. From the *tricolore* cockade to the angle of the chopping blade, the symbols of the overthrow of the Old Order were intended to obliterate the political and cultural memory of all that had come before.

In "People Church" mythology, re-invented nightly by sleepless parish council chairpersons, the very notion of an unelected and maybe even (horrors) ordained person occupying the head chair is not only undemocratic, it is not collegial, not communal, not compassionate, not sharing, caring enough. The usurper who earns that chair will do so only with the consent of the majority, or, as is customary with one-person, one-vote democratic processes, with the support and approval of the most capable power group eyeing the throne. In "People Church," that means women.

Until 1988, my only curiosity about the women's movement in the Church was my puzzlement over why so many liturgy committees were headed by a chairperson whose husbandperson had just left her. And why all liberated nuns were aggressive, unbending, anti-male and anti-hierarchial. And why they kept in their midst one of those coy, avidly agreeable clergymen with blindfolded mentality, except when the Sisterhood sent him off to Aruba or Cancun to give his act a rest at Club Med.

St. Joseph's "People Church" boasts a woman homilist who takes over the pulpit regularly with the full acquiescence of the Oblates. St. Joseph's is home to women advocating change within the Church in Canada and remonstrating for more active roles than those women pursued in the past. This is the natural result of the feminist movement that has swept

North America for the last two decades extending its reach into the Church, the same feminist movement that has drawn so many nuns out of the convent and into the sanctuary with a whirlwind of ad libbed liturgical experimentations. Inclusive language is their battle cry.

The Mutilation Ministry

The mutilation ministry takes over here, scissors in hand, snipping off the masculine identifiables from every thought, word and deed in the Scriptures all the way back to heaven.

When errors of the past have been corrected and the true identity of the Twelve Apostolettes is determined, then the priesthood will be where it belongs, in the hands of those persons best suited to totalitarianism, the matriarchs of the New World Order. The bishops, ever in tune with prevailing trends, will excoriate any unsharing, uncaring "being non-persons" who do not celebrate the Goddess they serve. And at the rate things are going, all that could happen next Monday.

The Liturgical Dance Ministry

One staged liturgical production of several years ago begged to be dubbed "Lay Ministers on Broadway" or "New Faces of 1982." It took place in St. Andrew's Church, Thunder Bay.

Across the steps of the altar a line of young women in long white shifts with angel sleeves gestured and posed, as another line of white-shifted women danced up the aisle. Once again, the faithful were overwhelmed with the mind-numbing infantilism of a parish council gone mad with nursery school theatre.

But it was not to end there. At the start of his homily, the "presider" priest asked everyone in the church to take something off and pass it to someone they did not know. Watches, gloves, scarves were passed haltingly between people who were either too confused or embarrassed to   make   eye-contact with

another. At the end of the homily, the priest invited everyone
to retrieve their items, during which exchange he explained
the virtue of giving.

If ever I needed proof that the mass would be completely
stolen from right under the noses of the faithful without a
whimper of complaint, this was it. Not one voice was raised
in surprise or disgust. Like sheep, they allowed themselves to
be experimented with and were made foolish in the bargain.

To avoid taking part in this nonsense, I stepped into the
aisle and walked to the vestibule. There I was surprised to
meet an old Jesuit I had known for years. He was dressed to
assist at mass but stood in the shadows, an expression of the
deepest grief on his face.

"Is this for real?" I asked him.

"I'm afraid so, Jim," he said. "I'm afraid so. And I'm just
plain afraid."

What has happened to the interior of St. Joseph's is a
direct result of simple, old-fashioned willfulness, of thumbing
the nose at tradition, at values, at laws, at the very order and
authority of the Church as reflected in the art, music and
architecture of Roman Catholicism. Its existence is proof that
the archbishop no longer has any right to meddle. If everything
a member of the Church does is considered a ministry, then
nobody is unique, Church authority is folded into the porridge
and, quicker than you can say "takeover," the hierarchy has
been levelled. And so the teaching ministry is joined by the
communications ministry to take their rightful place alongside
the ministry to gays and lesbians, the ministry of married ex-
priests and ex-nuns and the publications ministry.

The disorientation ministry made sure that there was
enough confusion in the Church to make all of the above sound
normal. It got an early start in 1962-65. The mutilation of the
language of the faith began in earnest at the Second Vatican
Council with the dusting-off of the word "liturgy." The
"sacrifice of the mass" became "the celebration of the
eucharist," "confession" became "reconciliation," and that
was just the beginning. The word "mass" was all but banned
from use in seminaries, colleges and schools. The "table of the
Lord," "spiritual banquet" and "community of believers"

appeared.

"Collegiality," "committee," "fellowship" led the way to the sharing, caring revolution. Now the silly season was in full bloom. Gender personhood (men and women) were no longer beings with maleness or femaleness, they were each "a being person." The sharing, caring "being person" was the new church-goer. In caring for their fellow being persons they would, without hesitation, share in the joy of projecting their newfound personhood on the archbishop himself should he ever invade their community.

In short, St. Joseph's typifies the collapse of the institution of the Church that was engineered by laity with weekend workshops on the liturgy, nuns with too many or too few classroom hours in social work, priests who call themselves feminists without any real knowledge of the needs of women in the Church and bishops who will do anything, anywhere, anytime if it will satisfy their long-suppressed desire to be just a teacher with a controllable, appreciative classroom.

Ever anxious to ensure that "unity in diversity" will end up on their epitaphs, most bishops, in the "spirit of Vatican II," have sacrificed what was unique and precious to Roman Catholicism in pursuit of that other buzz-word from the '60s, ecumenism. The reign of destruction unleased by Vatican II on the city's sacred interiors continues unabated. The art, music and architecture that nourished the faith for centuries has been desecrated in the name of modernity. Altars, communion rails, tabernacles, confessionals — the externals of Roman Catholicism's sacraments issuing from the death and Resurrection of Christ, are gone, as if Anglicans, Baptists, Methodists and Pentecostals would come rushing into the "One World People Church" as soon as all symbols of Roman Catholicism had been erased. Church and chapel have been made barren. The womb of the faith has been gutted. The Church has been scraped.

It was after such occasions as my tour of St. Joseph's, encountering yet more evidence of the madness that was shredding Roman Catholicism, that I would often make my way back to Champlain on his rocky promontory and spend time in his shadow looking upriver, imagining the rapids and chutes and cataracts that nourished this country to its fertile greatness, and there I would remember ...

Is it immoral to want what once was? What if it's needed again? What about yearnings for innocence? What about aspirations? What about art? What about beauty? What about ritual? Without them, the language of life can be nonsense for some.

Revisiting a squeaky pew might be just the answer right now if saints and martyrs and God are your heritage. Why can we not smell incense again, inhale that precious fragrance and dream of the perfumes of heaven? Because people don't commit acts of worship any more, acts of — it's almost too embarrassing to say — adoration!

Oh, it's better now. They still get together on Sundays and sing and shake hands and feel good and commune — yes, that's a good word for it, they commune with one another. It's like a picnic, sort of. Nice really.

Please! Don't give me sociology. Don't give me theology. Just give me back the wonder of my youth. Give me a true reminder of my littleness before God. Let me enjoy the sight of an altar boy being distracted by the picture of an angel.

The child targets God with ease. He simply fits himself as an arrow into a bow and flies back to the heart that gave him life. In dreams and in childhood we travel that way. But time slackens the bow. There are few bull's- eyes in middle age.

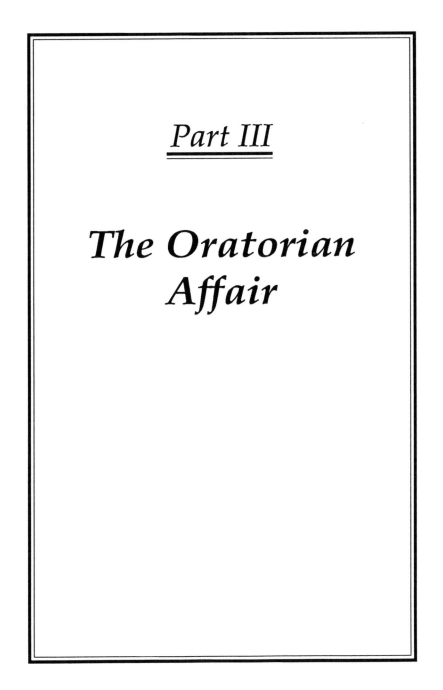

Part III

The Oratorian Affair

1

Romanesque Victorian Gothic Ironic

Ironies abound in the physical setting that housed the Oratorians.

It was designed by architect J.R. Bowes in response to the tastes and ideologies of the late Victorian period.[1] In an era when a Gothic revival was heavily influencing residential and commercial designs, another revival was also in the air, the recurring controversy of ultramontanism, which pitted those who defended the authority of the central Church in Rome against those who pushed for regional autonomy. Bowes left no doubt as to where his loyalties lay, designing in the exterior steeple the unmistakable silhouette of the papal tiara, then repeating that symbol of papal authority on no less than nine pinnacles of the high altar and two side altars.

Reinforcing the historic loyalties of the Irish to the Church, he chose in the east- and west-facing stained-glass windows to present not the Gospel scenes then being challenged and mutated by the theologians of the day, but rather a display of symbols deeply rooted in the faith that over the centuries had also become a veritable litany of Irish identity: the Sacred Heart, the Immaculate Heart, the Trinity triangle framing the eye of God, the lamb, the cross, the harp. Fleurs-de-lis, shamrocks and holy cross heather figure repeatedly in the high

valance of Bowes's sanctuary, window trim and double borders
banding the interior. Polychrome mitre-shaped spandrels
separated the fans of the high vault, reinforcing again the
message of Creation, Redemption and Sanctification.

The architect, steadfast in his vision, must have imprinted the
very will to survive upon these walls, for St. Brigid's, unlike
so many sanctuaries looted and pillaged in the '70s, still
retains its high altar.

Now described as Romanesque Victorian Gothic, St.
Brigid's represents a heritage already centuries old.[2] Unlike
the textures, lush detail and lavish furnishings of Notre Dame,
the interior of St. Brigid's, from soaring, high-vault fans to the
stark simplicity of the stone-block wall patterns, echoes the
state of so many of Ireland's churches impoverished of their
movable heritage during the purges of abbeys and monasteries
in the seventeenth century. St. Brigid's decorations and
furnishings were designed to be immovable, from the Nativity
and Crucifixion murals painted directly onto linen then
cemented onto wall surfaces, to the uncarpeted floors, the oak
strips of which point forward to the single and only focus of the
entire design, the tabernacle of the high altar.

Nevertheless, all of that virtually disappeared from view
two decades ago. In the hippie-dippy Church delirium of the
'60s and '70s, during the wholesale burglarization of church
interiors by priests, nuns and the laity following Vatican II, the
entire church was painted grey. Not even Cromwell in his
savage romp through the churches of Ireland was imaginative
enough to consign the symbols of the faith to whitewashed
oblivion. That act of horrific vandalism was the work of nuns
and priests whose Vatican II "high" blinded them to the
primary colours.

Did only the Catholics paint their churches grey? How
and when did it happen? How long was I looking the other
way? It seems like only yesterday we said "*Et cum spiritu
tuo.*"

Labourers, tradesmen, merchants, scholars, mayors and
prime ministers called St. Brigid's theirs for most of its
history.[3]

In 1905, former Ottawa mayor Samuel Bingham's

funeral saw five hundred of Ottawa's finest gentlemen in full mourning accompany one hundred horse-drawn carriages that left St. Brigid's to lead him to Notre Dame Cemetery.[4]

The following year, his wife travelled to Rome and returned with the high altar cross currently on view, having had it blessed by Pope Pius X, the same pope who identified and condemned Modernism in 1907 as "the synthesis of all heresies."[5]

For some eight decades from the date of its building, St. Brigid's parish flourished in sickness and in health. It flourished also as common ground for the French and the English, attracting those families who thought themselves not necessarily poor but certainly not of the class of Church supporters who overflowed the collection plates each Sunday at the basilica up the way. Both rich and otherwise walked shoulder to shoulder on feast days, like the Feast of Corpus Christi, with banners aloft, candles alight, past decorated houses, toward that house chosen from year to year for the honour of hosting an outdoor mass in its yard.

St. Brigid's was designated a "territorial parish," and much would be made of this term by the anti-Traditionalist campaigners who blamed the Oratorians for ignoring the local parish and playing to a wider audience. But the fact of the matter is, by the time the Oratorians arrived, the parish had shrunk to several families.

To build the bridge across the Ottawa River, connecting Ottawa with Hull, Quebec, and to create the parkland along Sussex Drive where the offices of the Department of External Affairs now stand, the powers that be expropriated that entire section of Lowertown which, from 1857 to 1920, was designated with the letter "O" on Ottawa maps. The area was nicknamed by the French "Le Lot 'O'."[6] Hundreds of families were bought out in what is remembered with bitterness as a ruthless, unfeeling manipulation of the population by the governing body of the time.

With Lot "O" went much of the "territorial parish" that made up St. Brigid's. The church's coffers were depleted, the morale of the parish devastated. So stood St. Brigid's in the '60s when the resident priest of the time, a man who kept a large, cross dog at the door of the rectory to keep parishioners away, had workmen take paint rollers to the interior of the church and virtually demolish every indication of its identity as an "Irish and others" church.

Then in 1987, into a decrepit, vandalized Ottawa church, barren as the laughing Sarah, came that massive infusion of creativity — four Oratorian priests, and with them five Brothers studying for the priesthood.

One of their first undertakings was the restoration of the vandalized interior. One of the Brothers recalled the enormity of the task.

"When we arrived at St. Brigid's, we saw a once magnificent building that had been devastated. A project was already underway with the Ontario Heritage Foundation. Most of their money was spent on keeping the building from falling apart. Only now are we able to look at the building and come up with some solution for restoring the interior.

"Our first intention was to restore the murals that had been covered with grey paint. We employed two restoration artists who had worked down the street restoring the Rideau Chapel in the National Gallery of Canada."[7]

Ash- and oak-covered sanctuary walls, for two decades buried under grey-green latex, were stripped bare to do once more what the architect intended — catch the sun and warm to a glow the oak communion rail and the butternut pews. The half-acre of green carpet was lifted to reveal golden oak floors in the aisle and sanctuary, acoustically hardening the interior and accentuating each note from the 1910 Cassavante organ. The pipes of the organ were umbrellaed with plastic to stop the disintegrating latex of the ceiling from filtering into the organ's innards.

Palestrina made an instant comeback. A Gallery Choir of thirty voices was followed by the Children's St. Brigid's Choristers of twenty. The Collegium Musicum of eight voices studied and performed selected masterpieces. A Gregorian Chant course, a Latin for the laity course, catechism, a men's oratory and women's oratory were all underway by the end of the first season.[8] As Virginia Byfield wrote in *The Western Report*, the faithful were instructed and coached in the reformed

Vatican II liturgy of the Novos Ordo Mass; major features were sung in Latin with Palestrina motets as is the custom of the order founded in 1575 by St. Philip Neri. (Neri was Palestrina's confessor.)

Like Oratorian congregations elsewhere, this one was quickly famous for its ability to pray or sing aloud the *Kyrie*, *Gloria*, *Credo*, *Sanctus* and *Agnus Dei*.

Occasionally, the organ was accompanied by the cello, and other times a string section would greet those arriving for the rosary and benediction on the thirteenth of every month. Sunday evening Vespers chanted in solemn Gregorian attracted women and, notably, men who had not opened their mouths to sing in church since they were school age.

The bank of altar boys reached twenty-eight in number. Exposition of the Blessed Sacrament occurred all day Sunday.

The Brothers ran the business end of the parish from computer-equipped offices on the below-ground floor. The Fathers made themselves available at all times for hearing individual confessions. With four priests, five brothers and twenty-eight altar boys, lay men and women were not called upon to distribute the eucharist. But there were lay readers at the Sunday 9 a.m. mass.

The pace was relentless. The enthusiasm for the Oratorians came from all age groups. Perhaps one reason for their popularity was, in a Church that for three decades had been struggling to evolve social programs for the poor and the homeless, the momentum of the Oratorians clearly revealed a refreshing strategy for uplifting the depressed community. The Oratorian pursuit of excellence in music and the arts had sown the seeds of nothing less than an artistic and cultural revival of that part of Lowertown. In less than a year, Father Ashley and the Oratorians were awarded a special citation by Ottawa City Hall for their work in heritage restoration. Writers, musicians, artists and filmmakers came to take a look. "It was the success of St. Brigid's that made it so offensive," Father Ashley would conclude.

But their success was more than just superficial. When a Secretary of State official, in response to an application by a parishioner to secure support for a written history of the Irish builders of St. Brigid's, came to view a mass one Sunday, he reported his surprise at meeting Ethiopians, Jamaicans, Trinidadians, Peruvians, Filipinos, Koreans and Lebanese in the congregation. The Oratorians were revealing in their choice of music, ceremony and solemnity those universal ingredients which once were the hallmark of Roman Catholicism.

If priests had to be rated on Vatican II report cards, the Oratorians, certainly as far as music was concerned, would have received straight As.

Duane Galles, a musician and writer for the St. Paul Minnesota publication *Sacred Music*, noted that the Oratorians were doing the unheard-of, fulfilling to the letter articles of the Sacrosanctum Concilium on music from Vatican II: Article 112, that the treasury of sacred music be preserved and cultivated for the glory of God and sanctification of the faithful — Check. Article 114, that choirs be diligently developed — Check. Article 115, that musicians be given liturgical training — Check. Article 116, that Gregorian Chant, being proper to the Roman liturgy, be given pride of place — Check. Article 15, that pastors see to it that the faithful are able to say or sing in Latin those parts of the ordinary of the mass belonging to them — Check.[9]

At St. Brigid's, the Oratorians and the faithful ensured that music was "integral to the solemn liturgy" as the Sacrosanctum Concilium states.

Something long awaited had happened here.

For two decades, the mass had been cocooned from clear view within a swirl of folk guitars, burlap slogan banners and the mind-numbing banality of pop liturgy, as if the surest way to appeal to the largest audience while avoiding anything that might irk the critics was to adopt the hallmark mediocrity of television programming. Out went the "sacrifice." Out went "the mass." Out went "holy."

But now, here, at the Oratory, after a long, imposed larval stage, the great prayer of the mass had emerged complete, brilliant in design, breathtaking in display, to take flight with the hearts and minds of people starved for truth, goodness and beauty. The Oratorian mass was an act of worship of the highest quality. Every gesture made, every word intoned, every note of music played was done so lovingly and fully attended to by the participants on the altar, in the choir and in the pews. All led forward, ever forward, from the Upper Room, over Gethsemene, up the Via Dolorosa to the first altar, Calvary.

At the first service I attended I recognized once again with joyous elation the holy sacrifice within the mass, that fraction of time when you are elevated above your very nature, that instant of union with the One who, invisible through all Eternity, took on a child's flesh to become visible in and conquer time. I knew that instant of truth when in the heart and in the mind you are momentarily more than you were. And the brilliance and the glitter leaves you dazzled. And you remember a time when somebody was in charge, when you knew who you were and where you came from and what you were destined for.

And just when the heart, mind and soul had been filled to capacity by the multilayered nourishment of this mass, they were made to overflow when, instead of abandoning the sanctuary to the comparative gloom of the midday sun, the celebrant raised onto the high altar a glittering monstrance, framing at its golden centre the fruit of the womb, the Upper Room, Golgatha and the empty tomb – perfect purity, perfect peace, the perfect sacrament. After years of searching liturgical maps for the X that marks the spot, I was home.

How on earth had the Oratorians come to be in this, the most liberal diocese in Canada? And how had they, by the summer of 1988, survived here already for twelve months? Downstairs, after mass, amidst the din of a hundred conversations and the carry-on of countless kids, Father Ashley detailed their origins.

"In the devotions we had once a month in the church where I was a pastor in British Columbia, we would gather to say the rosary with the lay people, hear confession and have a procession of the Blessed Sacrament.

"It occurred to us that we were working well together, even though the other three priests just came to help out. Also, we had a number of young people who were attracted to the type of work we were doing.

"We thought there must be some way of formalizing the type of life we seemed inclined to lead. We got together to discuss the whole matter and eventually invited the Superior of the Toronto Oratory to come to Vancouver to meet Archbishop Carney on our behalf." (Toronto's Oratory serves its immediate neighbourhood of soup kitchens, hospital and welfare families with success while drawing devoted support from individuals in parishes far and wide.)

"Carney wasn't favourable to the idea of an Oratory within his diocese but said he would give us permission to seek out another bishop who might be willing to allow us to establish an Oratory.

"The other priests said, well, there's no way that we will be accepted in any diocese to form an Oratory. But lo and behold, in August of 1986, a letter arrived at the front office, I opened it up with two other priests and it was from Archbishop Plourde inviting us to Ottawa!"[10]

2

Invitation To A Theme Park

A humble soul once, sensing the cause of her superior's enduring despair, pierced the gloom with, "If you've lost God, pray to the Three Wise Men. They will lead you back. They know the way."

Was it fatigue with the gloom that prompted Archbishop Plourde on August 5, 1986, to write to four British Columbia priests:

"It is my earnest desire to see a Congregation of the Oratory of St. Philip Neri formally erected in the Archdiocese of Ottawa. It is my intention to give you a parish with a large rectory which would be the centre of your religious life but which would allow you to serve the diocese according to its needs."[1]

St. Philip Neri, "the Apostle of Rome" would have fit right in with the Magi.[2]

As Father Ashley explained, "In his lifetime he emphasized the beauty of the liturgy and the proper adornment of the Church. He imparted the belief that God should be worshipped in fitting surroundings. Thus we should do as much for the glory of God as we can."[3]

Plourde could not plead ignorance of the meaning and means of order of an Oratory of St. Philip Neri. To invite them to Ottawa, allot them a specific parish and allow them to direct the education and spiritual life of five novices could not possibly be done offhand, in the dark, or in ignorance of the effect they were likely to have on the near-empty parish selected for them. That they would attract parishioners from other parishes, even from outside the city, was obvious. That is the fate of the Oratory wherever it exists. It is an oasis of excellence in liturgy and music.

I can see no other reason behind Plourde inviting them to Ottawa than that he desired this very thing in his archdiocese. It was not the ability to attract the faithful from far and near that he underestimated; he must have known that would happen. It was his own archdiocese that he misread. Having allowed the liberal left full reign in his diocese, he was now to learn of their power.

With his retirement imminent, Plourde might have seen the Oratorians as a further dimension to the "diversity" that he was so proud of, one that would re-establish a modicum of sobriety in the Catholic Disney-ride Ottawa had become. Under Plourde, the archdiocese of Ottawa had become a Teilhard de Chardin theme park for the liberal left, where the Ten Commandments had been replaced by two slogans: "unity in diversity" came to mean "anything goes" as long as it is not in Latin and not Roman and "in the spirit of Vatican II." The invocation of Vatican II was used to legitimize the acting out of fantasies by a privileged, spoiled and wilful religious class. This included a dean advocating to his seminarians that searching for social interaction in gay bars could possibly be a fulfilment of one's priestly function; that anal intercourse, if indulged in unselfishly, could possibly be a source of virtue; "Dignity" masses, where practising homosexuals could receive the sacraments in the "compassionate spirit of Vatican II." Nuns holding hands in a circle and dedicating themselves to Mother Earth.

One could be forgiven for suspecting that, with his invitation to the four Oratorian priests, Plourde, in the closing years of his archbishopric, was seeking to leave a deposit of traditionalism as a guide to the long-suffering hard-core of faithful alienated by the silly goings-on of an out-of-control elite within the city's religious community.

If that was the case, then inviting the Oratorians to Ottawa was an act of quiet courage by a secure, determined archbishop.

Alas, his resulting actions indicate that he was completely out of touch with the reality of his empire. Quick, someone, a coat to cover the emperor.

Under Plourde, the bureaucracy of the Church in Ottawa swelled to become an estate of its own, firmly in the hands of the liberal left. With the weakening of hierarchical authority that followed Vatican II, a furious grab for power saw nuns and priests in Ottawa, as elsewhere, racing through universities, snatching up degrees and staking out their professional territory within the Church with executive skill and military thoroughness.

By the 1980s the archdiocese of Ottawa was overstaffed and over-educated, a great buzzing hive of specialists, completely out of touch with Catholicism. And at their centre was an archbishop whose reputation had long ago been founded on, above all else, his perennial compulsion for acting out, role-playing the delinquent wherever Rome was concerned.

Adding an extra and completely artificial importance to their machinations was the fact that in this city was located, literally at the archbishop's back door, the building that housed the Canadian Conference of Catholic Bishops. And what more logical location for the National Action Committee on the Status of Women than Ottawa, where the reality of a wartime ratio of five women to every man is seldom forgotten. Ottawa is, indeed, as Virginia Byfield pointed out in *The Western Report*, "the country's radical feminist capital."[4] The bishops of Canada, to a man intimidated by the feminist movement within the Church, have allowed the Conference Centre to become a high-profile fem-thought bunker.

Egos careening madly out of control, the bishops repeatedly stupefy governments and the press by acting as though Christ had gathered fishermen together to teach them about trade unions. What with the bishops congregating regularly in Ottawa to promulgate bulls on El Salvador, unemployment, South African apartheid and other headline-grabbing causes about which they can know little and upon which their influence must surely be mostly imaginary, the mood of the archdiocese is that this is where it is all happening, that this is the front line, the cutting edge, the place to be.

That, of course, means limousines and power lunches and banquets with groaning boards, coy peek-a-boo games with the press, the usual smattering of platitudes about the hungry and the homeless followed by some eccentric action that leaves the public numb with disbelief. One such step was Plourde's real estate deal with the People's Republic of China. In an era when the much-touted ecumenical movement is being destroyed by the transfer of public high schools to Catholic school boards, Plourde sold a magnificent facility, a former historic convent school, to the Chinese for use as an embassy.

One wonders what trials the Wise Men endured after depositing at the feet of the new-born king their gold, frankincense and myrrh. History cannot define the countries of their origin so one cannot ascertain to what regions they returned, but clearly, since no tidal wave of curiosity-seekers made their way to the spot where the star stopped over Bethlehem, it seems certain they chose not to promote their findings.

Church history is filled with men and women who suffered for the truths of the faith. In this century alone there stand the names of three men who spent the better part of a hundred years faithfully reading the designs of heaven. The light in their sky was the innocence of Catholic truth. Steadfastly refusing to bargain with shadows, they were denied, censored or excommunicated. Throughout it all, their tortured paths converged in their defence of the belief that the teaching authority of the Church comes from God.

Cardinal Mindszenty rejected any compromise with atheistic communism and suffered imprisonment for his stance, only to be demoted by Paul VI. Padre Pio, the stigmatist, living out his priesthood as a living, bleeding crucifix, year in and year out fulfilled his priestly mandate by consoling penitents throughout endless hours in the close confines of the confessional, only to be silenced and quarantined. Then, Archbishop Marcel Lefebvre, for his relentless defence of the Immemorial Mass, earned the enmity of the Modernists, which brought him ultimately to excommunication. Love them or hate them, cheer them or jeer them, their fidelity to the Incarnate Wisdom makes brilliant the narrow road out of the twentieth century.

The first Sunday the Oratorians proceeded up the aisle toward the high altar of St. Brigid's must surely have sent shudders through the Modernists in the congregation. The vestments worn were not the trendy unisex caftans being modelled on the runways of the other churches in town. They were pre-Vatican II soutanes and surplices and birettas. They must indeed have appeared as threatening alien life forms to those in the pews who, for the last twenty-five years, had ordered their lives according to their own conscience. What an affront those classic vestments must have presented to those for whom the Church began with Vatican II, those in the pews that day who had expunged from their minds anything dated pre-1960.

Had these pillars of the New Church been versed in the authentic texts of Vatican II, they would have soon realized the Oratorians were following their directives conscientiously. But how many of us have immersed ourselves in those authentic texts? Once the pre-conciliar Church was cut off, set adrift like an old barge full of useless antiques, many traumatized priests and nuns succumbed to the claptrap of the '60s — anti-authoritarianism; sexual, social and spiritual liberation; self-aggrandizing, self-centred, self-serving. They had a Church-sanctioned slogan that, like pixie-dust, kept their fragile self-images afloat in never-never-land — "the spirit of Vatican II" — and none of that promoted the notion of reading the manual to see how the newfangled device would work. After all, the performance of Mother Mary Ignition's new Ford van hardly depends on the driver or passenger understanding the engine.

Alas, you only get one chance to make a first impression. The Oratorians' cause was lost the first day they walked up the aisle in procession. They were living, breathing reminders of an authoritarian, dogmatic past that had to be kicked lifeless at all costs until it could be buried once and for all.

That Sunday, before they reached the high altar, the campaign to get them out had begun. That campaign would continue day in and day out, an unstoppable and unalterable demonstration of the determination of the "People Church" advocates agitating for an altar they could control.

By June 30, 1988, the Oratorians had been in Ottawa only twelve months when far off in Switzerland, Archbishop Lefebvre proceeded with the consecration of his bishops and was excommunicated. Immediately, in Ottawa, Joseph Aurèle Plourde, archbishop, dispatched to the Oratorians the letter telling them to get out. The battle between the Traditionalists and the Modernists was to be brought home under cover of the darkness that had descended on the Church that day.

3

The Golden Boot Award

It came by courier. Father Ashley was sitting in the confessional when one of the novices approached and handed him the letter.

It was dated June 30, 1988, the day of the Lefebvre excommunication. It read:

"After much consultation, reflection and prayer, I have finally come to a decision concerning the future of your community in the diocese.

"It has become apparent, after the trial period of a year, that the approach which your community has taken and wishes to continue to pursue is a source of friction in the diocese. (Then came the paragraph lifted right out of the Teilhard 101 primer.)

"The presence of the Oratorians has been a cause of division in our midst. I know that there is diversity here. But when a certain type of diversity causes friction and disagreement, we no longer have unity in diversity but division. In view of the importance of unity for Church communion, I cannot tolerate that.

"Moreover, we are not able to offer you the kind of situation you are seeking in order to carry out your ministry. As you have said yourself, your dream would be to live together day in and day out and serve the people who would come to you freely and to accept more priests and students. This is not possible here.

"I have, therefore, decided, after consultation with the Council of Priests, that given our experience during this trial period, that I cannot approve the establishment of an Oratory in the Archdiocese. Consequently, I am asking you to find another diocese where the conditions may be more favourable for the establishment of an Oratory or return to the diocese in which you are incardinated. I realize that this may take some time, but I would like to appoint a new pastor to St. Brigid's no later than July 1, 1989 at which time your appointment as administrator would be revoked.

"I am sorry if this decision causes you grief; I appreciate the dedication, hard work and good things which you have done, but having considered all the aspects of this pastoral situation, I truly see no other alternative. If you want to discuss this with me, I will be happy to do so at your convenience.

Yours truly in Christ

Joseph Aurèle Plourde
Archbishop of Ottawa."[1]

The mild tone of this letter reminds me of the quiet that came just after the whistle of a V-2 rocket and just before the explosion.

But the point was made loudly enough. The Oratorians, after a year of sacred heritage restoration, revival of Gregorian Chant and the development of popular programs in liturgy and music, were the honoured recipients of what Father Ashley would call "the golden boot award."

The strain of a year of uncertainty showed as Father Ashley described the reaction of the Oratorians to the expulsion notice.

"The news was devastating to all of us, especially considering the fact we were invited here. We had travelled three thousand miles across Canada, moved all our belongings, on the strength of the letter we received from Archbishop Plourde.

"We never expected any such thing would happen. We never were so naïve as to think that there would be absolutely no problem, but surely we are a new community. We expected we had a minimum of five years and after that to take a look at what needed to be done.

"It really has been rather shabby.

"We have suffered tremendously. I don't know if people realize what it's like with this hanging over our head. Nowhere to go. One minute we are offered something, the next thing, it's off.

"We try to resign ourselves to what God has asked us to suffer but we're not seeking out suffering, that's for sure."[2]

Plourde's timing was intended to hammer the Oratorians into oblivion by making of their expulsion a mirror image of the showdown between Lefebvre and Rome. In the process, it was sure to damage their reputations irretrievably by implying disobedience on their part. Nothing could be further from the truth.

The efforts that went into the ruin of the Oratorians were methodical, vicious, vindictive and totally personal. A pampered, fussed-over, catered-to religious and laity who for two decades had been reinventing the Church in their own image had come face to face with the unthinkable — priests who were not conforming to the rules of behaviour so long adhered to by the cowed and emasculated priesthood of the 1980s.

Those rules of behaviour were firmly set. No longer could priests counsel on the means by which their flock would get from this world to the next. Thanks to the parish councils, women's lobbies, liberated Sisterhood and ecumenism, Catholics could now use their priest to define for themselves a more comfortable place in this world.

Correspondence from the conspirators began hitting the Archbishop's desk before the Oratorians were unpacked. (They would never get a chance to fully unpack.)

The first shock to the Oratorians was the identity of the people behind it.

"The major opposition came from nuns who took petitions door to door," explained Virginia Byfield, "other nuns who wrote the archbishop from as far away as ninety miles [Pembroke] and certain non-parish professional people who saw the order as reactionary."[3]

Among the non-parish professionals referred to were a few lawyers. The part they played in the anti-Oratorian letter writing was to be pivotal, not for legal reasons, but because of the elitism evident in their correspondence. One may assume that they came to St. Brigid's because they could not get a handle on what was happening in their own parishes. Fair enough — nothing could be more normal in a city setting than to gravitate toward a church you find bearable. But this same non-parish factor, while composing the majority of complaints to Archbishop Plourde, would deny to the rest of the Oratorian congregation, some of whom travelled weekly from as far away as fifty miles, the same consideration.

The effort to demolish the Oratory might have come to very little if it had not been fuelled by one specific source — those nuns committed to the liberal cause. In their opposition to the Oratorians, a certain cross-section of nuns displayed seemingly inexhaustible energy.

Do not confuse this with religious fervour or willing martyrdom. This was just the Church's militant nouveau activists, the easy-to-manipulate, unveiled troops. They jackbooted about the parish with the zeal of foot soldiers in a holy war, burning off energy they had once squandered in the cloister. They scurried about in a mirthless frenzy, incapable of talking about anything else but getting the Oratorians out of Ottawa. That these individuals considered themselves natural candidates for a women's priesthood is no surprise; they were already infallible. They saw the Oratorians as traditionalists, ultra-conservative, right wing, reactionary, fanatic, with only one goal — to return the Church to the male hierarchial domination of the Dark Ages.

This opposition was soon operating out of St. Joseph's Church, where they had free reign, the Oblates in that parish living up to their long-standing reputation of being easy to manipulate. From there, the Sisterhood networked to other parishes, applying pressure to other priests and parish councils on the issue that mattered most — consolidating opposition to the Oratory.

Alas, in the Oratorian affair, the man in authority was a pathetic figure, an aging archbishop, self-image spinning madly out of control, spiralling ever higher and higher on his own manic ego, being manipulated and ultimately robbed of the credibility of his office by the fem-thought bureaucrats surrounding him and applauding his every eccentricity.

The time and energy spent by the Sisterhood writing letters and collecting signatures for petitions was quite impressive, and one would have concluded their active number to be much higher than it was.

Everyone, from the most cynical media hack to the most naïve introvert in the pew, had a perfect working knowledge of just what motivated the Sisterhood: power. To achieve that, they were exterminating all potential opposition in advance.

How the Oblates who aided and abetted could for one moment believe these new amazons had any intention of sharing their sanctuary with men has always been a cause of considerable bewilderment to me.

4

Something Franciscan

During the year following the notice of eviction, the number of worshippers at St. Brigid's appeared to grow in direct proportion to the furore raised in the media by the brutally callous order of exile. Some special image of this minority of believers was being transmitted through newspaper and television reports that attracted individuals from every walk of life, every class, every level of education and every age.

One had to worship at St. Brigid's to perceive the prime ingredient of that special image. I think it was something Franciscan in their attitude. As believers, they all seemed to share a like stature, as if each upon entering had left all pretensions at the door, all worldly ways, pride in attachments, competitiveness, ambition, ego. Those who were attracted there seemed to undergo some invisible spiritual debriefing at the portals and entered impoverished of the world. Humility — that is what they shared. Is it any wonder that in a celebrity-crazed world they were hated?

I wonder if Bernadette was a Franciscan. She came often to mind that year as I watched young people, in admirable numbers and with remarkable constancy, actively involve themselves in the workings of the Oratory. In a world obscenely warring against the innocence of youth, the Oratory became a sanctuary for the beautiful reality of teenagers struggling with the awkwardness, shyness, dreaminess and downright goofiness that comes from inhabiting bodies growing, changing and developing beyond their control. There is something holy about that time in a teenager's life when he or she feels homely, useless and stupid.

Bernadette's yielding to those inevitabilities comes down to us across the century in a conversation she had with Monsignor Forçade after she left Lourdes. The Monsignor asked, "Is it true, Sister Marie Bernard, that you are good for nothing?" To which Bernadette answered, "I told you that myself, at Lourdes, when you were trying to persuade me to enter the community [convent}, and you said it didn't matter."[1]

And at another time, when being scolded because her illness kept her from doing her share of work in the convent, she answered with words that could be an anthem for anyone feeling put-upon by the stress of being a teenager: "It is my job to suffer."[2]

There is for me, in Bernadette's character, a perfect enactment of the sublime words of John the Baptist who commented about his own future role in the wilderness after recognizing Jesus as the Lamb of God, "I must decrease, so He may increase."

In those words, I find the best description of the individual who came to St. Brigid's, one who humbled himself, one who willingly, gladly, eagerly left his increase at the door so God could have a free hand with him.

Is it any wonder indeed that in the individual-conscience-centred Church of the '80s hatred was churned out day after day, vilifying these worshippers as cultish, neurotic, reactionary?

To the Archbishop, also, these people did not represent "an authentic Christian Community." In a November 9, 1987, letter to the superior of the Oratory, in words clearly intended to be condemnatory, he wrote: "You have taken Saint Brigid's Parish and turned it into a type of shrine which caters to people in the region who have maintained a nostalgic longing for the past and who seek an atmosphere normally found in shrines which attract all sorts of pilgrimages."[3]

It was just one of the utterances that over the year would

measure how far removed from the lives of his parishioners this archbishop actually was. In the context of the late '80s, the statement revealed something else, something both unexpected and embarrassing — stupidity at the top.

For a decade, people had been searching for stability by reassessing the norms and formulas for civilized behaviour. In radio and television, nostalgia for the '50s saw a veritable reliving of the music, styles and attitudes of that innocent decade. Ethnic culture and multicultural values were scrutinized with fascination by politicians, educators and artists searching for form and substance. In a world tyrannized by rapidly evolving communications techniques, strategies and experiments, people sought grounding in realities that amplified the actuality of their spiritual nature. And within the Church itself, the rediscovery and recovery of lost values was not only underway, it was already a trend. The unquestioning embrace of all that was new and trendy at the expense of all that was good and valued from the past was already an out-of-date, old-fashioned attitude. The arts world was spending millions restoring old theatres, and for a full decade governments had been allotting public funds for the restoration of old churches. Plourde and his bureaucratic menage of "liberated" nuns and trendy, power-conscious priests were not just stuck in the '80s; they never got out of the '60s.

In the '40s and '50s, as my brothers and sisters grew to twelve in number, being poor, being Catholic and being happy was considered a dangerous combination. Those happy in poverty because they knew in their souls that Rome was home were, however, considered potentially subversive.

Subversion was clearly what Plourde saw in the Catholics whom he accused of "nostalgia neurosis," Catholics who did not share the need for incessant novelty that had pushed parish council liturgies to the outer limits of sanity. The Oratorians preached and taught the magisterium. They were a constant reminder of how the archdiocese of Ottawa, under Plourde's direction, had reached the brink of no longer being in communion with Rome.

Plourde, of all people, should have understood subversion; subversion was what the '60s were all about. Call it anti-authoritarian, anti-Establishment, anti-form, call it liberation, renewal, call it what you like, the dominating theme of the '60s was not peace, love and flower-power, the two-finger peace sign was simply a way of giving order the finger twice. And that is precisely the state of mind of those nuns and priests who took wing from their vows in the '60s, and those who stayed in the nest to befoul it in the tiresome tradition of networking sophomoric campus rebellions against Rome on everything from liberation theology to homosexuality to women priests. At the head of that class was Joseph Aurèle Plourde, a little long in the tooth for hippiedom, perhaps, but is anyone ever too old for Disneyland?

Lest I leave you with the image of a benevolent old Peter Pan in Mickey Mouse ears, let me tell you a few things about the Archbishop's *modus operandi* that will make your candy floss congeal.

Plourde had as part of his arsenal two guilt trips designed to silence and humiliate anyone who challenged him or his smartly turned-out court. One was reserved for the media.

The local television and newspaper editors and reporters were not seduced by Plourde, his bureaucracy or his council of priests. They gave him what-for with gusto and a realistic reflection of the bizarre realities of his archdiocese. Both the Ottawa *Citizen* and the *Sun* adopted an attitude of respect and sympathy for the Oratorians and their congregation. This level-headed criticism was perhaps attributable to the fact that Plourde published his own newspaper. This publication, called *The Church in Ottawa Today*, was an unabashed vanity sheet staffed by Plourde's secretary, Patrick Powers. Powers filled this publication with columns of praise and flattery that would cause your sweet tooth to positively chalk over. In the grovelling vein of "We are so fortunate to have had you among us . . . " the paper printed column after column on Plourde's charity and far-sightedness and, from Plourde himself in the year leading up to his retirement, columns on "How you can honour me for my twenty-five years of service" (e.g. benefit dinners, roasts, bursaries carrying his name, etc.).[4]

Clearly, Plourde had intended to matter-of-factly edit the Oratorians out of his cartoon capers and leave them as nothing but faces on the cutting-room floor. But the media started splicing the snippets together.

Plourde's reaction was predictable. He accused the Oratorians and their congregation of leaking letters from his desk to the press and generally derided them for using the media. Then guilt trip number one was applied.

"The most elementary principles of charity would suggest that problems be discussed directly and privately and never in a public forum."[5]

Naturally enough, this admonition came after Plourde had discovered he could not use the media to his own advantage.

Guilt trip number two hinted darkly that "Many people would be profoundly offended."[6] It was applied in cases like this: When, in their "Petition of Recourse" to Rome appealing against Plourde's expulsion, the Oratorians listed "atrocities" (Plourde's word) that had taken place in his diocese, Plourde responded with "If I were to publish the arguments they used — many people would be profoundly offended." Then he added, "I wonder how many of our people would approve of the contents of this document?" If the document were submitted to the scrutiny of the gays, lesbians, pedophiles and would-be witch-priests who for two years had been announcing their presence in Ottawa in newspaper headlines, seminary curriculae, conferences and seminars, none naturally would have approved.

Plourde's demurring on "the elementary principles of Christian charity" and his caution that "people would be profoundly offended" fooled absolutely no one. That type of crook-and-mitre con game was all too similar to the "We have received your letter and will reply in due time" formula used when parents filed complaints about their child being molested, or "His Excellency cannot respond at this time because he is out of the archdiocese temporarily," which is what callers were told who were demanding action against the blatant alternate-lifestyle propaganda being served up by gay clerics in advance of a Dignity conference in the city.[7]

5

A Night At The Opera

The correspondence that flew to and from the Archbishop's office would have been too farcical even for Feydeau. The heights of silliness were scaled by the letter-writers searching for material for their petitions to the Archbishop. Assuming the tone of the grievously offended, the writers made it clear that they stood as the vanguard against any possible revival of "outdated spirituality." The very existence of their own modern spirituality, they seemed to say, was proof that Vatican II's entire purpose was not just to draw a line in the sand but to cause an earthquake that would perpetuate an ever-widening rift between old and new.

The purveyors of this "People Church" theory considered themselves the means by which the Church would continue to change until it was finally free standing, self-made. Any effort to oppose them in the slightest way would be quashed; not even the simplest challenge to their new absolutes would be allowed. Any attempt to acknowledge that there existed in the old anything of value would be halted immediately.

The words of the petitions leap off the page like lines of dialogue from a Marx Brothers movie. Especially fitted to read them would be Groucho's constant foil, the actress Margaret Dumont, in gown and pearls and upswept hairdo. When asked how she could keep a straight face while working with the comedians, she replied that it was easy because she couldn't understand a thing they were doing so never found them funny. She not only appeared bewildered, she *was* bewildered. I can almost hear her high-pitched New York accent reading the Archbishop's mail:

"One cannot expect altar boys to wear black shoes if they don't have any; it is difficult to be present in body and spirit at the Eucharist if one cannot see the altar because of suffocating clouds of incense, or when one worries about the fire damage to an old church because of 150 burning candles; it hurts ... when funerals are again celebrated in lots of black ... or when the celebration of Christian faith resembles that of a cult with lots of incense, red lights, secretive mumblings of public prayers, passive attendance, much genuflecting, plenty of candle light, an abundance of statues in the wrong places and museum pieces as vestments."[1]

That tour de force of priceless dialogue was written in a letter to the Archbishop dated January 7, 1988, five months after the Oratorians arrived. Accustomed to such petty stuffiness, Father Ashley delivered a few good lines of his own. [All commentaries from Father William Ashley are taken from *The Last Mass* video interview, taped July 1989].

"Do you throw away everything old? Do we throw old people away because they are old? Is something not good any more just because it's old? That's not to say new things can't be good and beautiful. The Church has always allowed for the use of new masterpieces of music and liturgy. But to automatically dismiss something merely because it's old, well, of course, that's ridiculous. If that's the case we throw away the Bible."[2]

That the letters to Plourde had appeared within weeks of the Oratorians' arrival presented something of a riddle. As Ashley explained:

"It seemed it happened so quickly after we arrived.

Perhaps it already had been planned. There was some type of attempt to have an orchestrated opposition to anything we might do. Perhaps there were some people lying in wait to find something to complain about. As soon as they had one little item they thought was significant they made use of it."[3]

It is evident that some of the comments came from people who had experienced neither the mysteries of the pre-Vatican II liturgy nor the beauty and purpose of the furnishing and externals of the sacraments. The organizers and promoters of the anti-Oratorian campaign clearly knew how to exploit these ill-informed alarms.

The following excerpts are taken from four letters written between September 20, 1987, and November 9, 1987:

"the old altar still stands against the wall!"[4]

"the fairly new altar which was reminiscent of a table has been replaced by a box-like structure which has floor length cloths and dressing."[5] (The thing "reminiscent of a table" was a baptismal font with a circle of plywood on top.)

"The interior of the church is like a carnival show."[6]

This put-down is aimed not only at the Oratorians' congregation but beyond them, at nineteen hundred years of devout faithful who hallowed such "carnival show" interiors with their supplications.

"I felt the priest didn't really care whether I was there or not."[7]

Now comes an effort at serious trouble-making.

"The whole atmosphere to me, seems as if it is a form of idolatry or cult."[8]

This masterpiece of duplicity comes directly from those

who were already choreographing "Women Church" liturgies extolling the virtues of Mother Earth.

Now begins the play on Vatican II buzz-words.

"The mass is more like a funeral than a 'celebration.'"[9]

And the alarm bell the liturgy cops always ring.

"The communicants received kneeling."[10]

An appalling ignorance also reveals itself and Plourde included this complaint on his list.

"The priest distributed communion with the prayer, 'Corpus Christi.'"[11]

But if you want to scare a bishop, start evoking Pius XII.

"The atmosphere is one of the late 1950s when the laity attended mass to watch the priests pray."[12]

That is odd. I went to mass all through the '50s and I never once thought of watching them pray.

The lethal slogans cannot be restrained for long. This is from a lawyer:

"Lowertown has become the home of the younger, upwardly mobile population. They were not evident in the congregation."[13]

Nothing will worry a trendy Canadian bishop in the 1980s like not appealing to the yuppies who keep trendy lawyers in business.

Then at last comes the threat.

"I will not return to St. Brigid's until the Oratorians are out."[14]

Duplicate copies of these letters were provided to the Oratorians by the Archbishop's office. The signatures were whited out, but strangely the address of the writer was left intact on the top right-hand corner of the page.

The letters, right down to the dotting of every "i" and the crossing of every "t", were tailored to intimidate an archbishop whose greatest fear was to be considered out of sync with "the spirit of Vatican II." Meanwhile, the organizers of the campaign to oust the Oratorians continued networking to other churches, parish councils and priests, preparing petitions to the archbishop.

But it was not so much the content of the letters nor their origin but the use to which they were put that raised the Oratorian affair from the level of a parish squabble to a stunning act of callousness that ultimately scandalized not just the participants but the entire archdiocese.

6

Dialogue Of The Oratorians

Is it possible to commit spiritual violence against a person? We understand about mental violence; we are subjected to it whenever someone decides to maim our self-confidence. But to do violence to the soul of a person must surely require a thorough working knowledge of the human spirit and its breaking point.

What I call an act of spiritual violence was committed against the Oratorians in July of 1989, one long year after the letter of expulsion from Archbishop Plourde was handed to Father Ashley as he sat in the confessional.

It came in the form of an eight-page *Information Bulletin* from the Office of the Archbishop on Kilborn Street, timed to be distributed to every church in the archdiocese to mark the date of the Oratorians' eviction, which had been set as no later than June 1, 1989.

Such was the sympathy for the Oratorians from the general public in Ottawa that their departure threatened to leave behind the image of men who had been mistreated, misled and martyred at the whim of the Archbishop. The

Information Bulletin was clearly intended to redress all that. It would, if it succeeded in meeting its author's goals, not just defeat the Oratorians, force them to give in and push them to the point of practically surrendering their principles, their orthodoxy, their traditionalism, their conversatism. The *Bulletin* would do more than drive a wedge between them and their supporters, possibly even drive wedges between them as individual priests and shatter their solidarity, their friendships. The *Bulletin*, if successful, would harm them. Harm them inside, lessen them spiritually, where no one but they could read the scars.

That the intention must have been such is indicated by the reaction the *Information Bulletin* drew from readers. It stunned them. People read it shaking their heads. Even opponents of the Oratory, even those who had no viewpoint one way or the other, knew that this was wrong. This was going too far. This was naked cruelty issuing from naked power.

Rumours abounded in the spring of 1989 that Plourde, his retirement imminent, had been relieved of part of his duties. The expected gossip about competence and failing health circled regularly. It is conceivable then, that the *Information Bulletin* was designed and executed not directly by Plourde but by the well-known and ill-regarded bureaucracy that thrived in his shadow. Such was the contempt in which his closest advisors were held that, had they not been so feared, they would have been challenged by just about every parish in the archdiocese.

The *Information Bulletin* was an exercise in deceit, a ruthless abuse of authority which, short of publishing notes taken in the confessional, could not have produced a more disheartening effect on parishioners. It was the act of a shepherd poisoning his flock. I will always hope that Archbishop Plourde was manipulated into publishing it. I cannot accept that he would terminate his career with the public annihilation of four good priests.

This eight-page, letter-sized *Information Bulletin* was one inch shy of matching the width of the guillotine blade that finally separated the unco-operative Carmelites from their habits. But it performed the same task — a lethal blade with eight sharp edges. For me, the day it struck, the Church in Ottawa was decapitated.

Never one to file away a compliment when xeroxing it would prolong its life, Plourde anchored the tone of his *Information Bulletin* by shamelessly including in it the following masterpiece of bootlicking, which arrived as part of one petition from the Modernist juggernaut.

> "It hurts us especially, since you yourself have been, over the years a consistent and inspiring prophet in leadership and practice in the spirit of renewal initiated by the Second Vatican Council."[1]

He also allowed himself to be held up as the wounded party by including this sympathetic note:

> "We are sad that what has been happening at Saint Brigid's over the past four months ... appears to nullify your own efforts as Chief Pastor of this Church in Ottawa."[2]

The letters made liberal use of every worn-out buzz-word, catch-phrase and slogan of the language of Vatican II: consensus, co-operation, community, consultant, guidance, advice, consent, collegiality, participation, presider, council — all of them spun in slick, implied threats.

To justify his actions, Plourde's Introduction to the *Information Bulletin* stated that "the most elementary principles of charity would suggest that problems be discussed directly and privately and never in public forum," but that he was forced to publish the *Information Bulletin* since "much media attention has been focused on a small group of individuals who sought public support for a group of four Vancouver priests ..."

Notice how the Oratorians, invited to establish an Oratory in Ottawa by Archbishop Plourde himself, are now represented as outsiders.

A tilting of the truth is emblematic of the smoke-and-mirrors con-game at which Modernists excel. It is why they are constantly on the spin, racing at breakneck speed from one speaking engagement to another, sending out a blizzard of petitions, flyers and leaflets, propelling their agenda at hurricane speed via endless seminars and touching down whenever and wherever possible to funnel out their manifestos through the media and a tidal wave of book publications by their pet theologians from printing houses they control. The purpose of all this frenzied activity is to keep the dust stirred up, lest it settle and the uncommitted see the reality of their game for what it is.

The body of the *Information Bulletin* catalogued letters of complaint sent to the Archbishop by the anti-Oratorian clique of "People Church" advocates, focusing on three letters in particular. These three letters map out quite clearly the strategy of the anti-Oratory forces and reveal the identity of those behind the power-grab in the archdiocese.

In the opening salvo, Plourde quotes from a letter dated September 21, 1987. The writer, supposedly a lay person very involved in parish councils, speaks directly to the Oratorians as if they were misbehaving juveniles.

"We understand you have not been in a parish in Ottawa for the last number of years and, as such, would benefit from the Parish Council's active assistance and guidance in monitoring the majority consensus of the parishioners who have been faithfully attending St. Brigid's Parish for several years."[3]

"We want only one priest on the altar, joined by a number of altar servers, both boys and girls, readers and eucharistic ministers: That the mass be said in English only in a relaxed and joyful atmosphere."[4]

No acknowledgment of the luxury of having four priests in one parish was offered. This seemingly innocuous little paragraph of demands exhibits perfectly how the meaning of the term "primacy of community" has degenerated to its current narrow meaning. The community of believers has been lost, and in its place "community" has come to mean the people who think like me and live between my house, the corner store and the sacristy. A small power group with control over "our liturgy," "our church," "our parish," could experience disorientation by going to mass just two blocks away from where they usually attend. Nothing exists or matters outside "our" little corner of the world. As for universal truths, well, what universe?

The challenge of that threadbare meanness of vision was one the Oratorians understood and countered. As Father Ashley explained:

"What we do here, I think, helps to broaden people's vision and not narrow it. The universal culture of the Church, the universal artistic values that the Church has to offer in her great music and her other traditions of art, these things are a tremendously enriching experience. They teach young people that there is more to the world than just my little area and so it helps overcome a certain narrowness of vision, a certain parochialism. We see people wanting to reduce everything to the local without any use whatever for looking at things in a more universal dimension.

"Just recently Pope John was interviewed by a number of reporters. They asked, 'What do you think is the fundamental problem in the church today,' and he answered by saying, 'The fundamental problem seems to be an over-emphasis on the local or particular church with a loss of vision of the universal Church and the value of seeing the universal Church as a means of safeguarding certain things.

"'Because we only live here in our particular situation, we can't see the value of things, it's the role of the universal Church to point that out to us. In some people's minds the local church is supposed to almost outweigh or obliterate the role that the universal Church and the central governing authority of the Church is supposed to play in relation to individual dioceses or individual local churches through the world.'"[5]

The letter-writer continues:

"We ask that the St. Brigid's family be welcomed at the beginning of the service."[6]

This demand for deference takes for granted that the community is now in charge. The demand is no less a threat than the withholding of applause by an audience until the entertainer grovels with feigned enthusiasm for their home town, place of work or sports team. ("How about those Maple Leafs?")

"We want the public address system and the lights turned on so our families can see the altar, hear the words of Our Lord and feel comfortable."[7]

The lights turned on? See the altar? Feel comfortable?

Bach, Mozart, Palestrina, a 1910 Cassavante organ, occasional cello and string quartets are dismissed with:

"We would like to ask Patrick back to play his guitar and sing songs that our children are familiar with."[8]

Ashley speaks here for everyone who has ever found himself speechless before a Claude Monet or swept away by Jessye Norman or Pablo Casals.

"Even if you set aside the whole idea of faith and religion in relation to the use of Latin or great works of music in the liturgy, who in heaven's name would ever want to be ignorant to these things? Why would anybody have such hatred for a language or for a certain type of music? I mean, wouldn't a broad cultural formation of youth imply that we don't want them to be raised in ignorance but we want them to have a broad cultural and spiritual perspective which would include the knowledge of Latin, of the tradition of the Church, of these great artistic and cultural monuments that the Church has bequeathed to us down through the centuries? Who in their right mind would want their children ignorant of these things?...

"If they see the elders throwing out things that seem so valuable, they say, well, why have respect for anything?

"Without reverence or respect we have nothing. That

means reverence and respect for the good of creative things that have been given to us by God, reverence and respect for the contribution of great artists and musicians down through the centuries. . . Not to have reverence for those things is to be less than appreciative of the gifts that God has given us."[9]

"We want to greet our families, friends and neighbours with the kiss of peace during that segment of the mass."[10]

Did the professional meddlers who got the kiss of peace from the early Church back into the mass really expect it was going to carry outside and warm the mean streets of our cities? Did they have some specific goal in mind other than distracting the faithful yet even more from the mass? Did they really expect those in the pews to find meaning in the long walk down the aisle by the smiling priest? Did they really imagine the contrived, transparent gesture was going to effect bonding among the faithful? If it disappeared from Christian gatherings in early Christian times, might there not have been a good reason?

Of all the clutter that has multiplied around the supposedly simplified celebration of the eucharist, none is less missed than the local variations on this inane charade when it is ignored.

"We do not want incense used at this liturgy!" [11]

This demand is a source of endless fascination for me.

As a boy, nothing transported me more quickly to the hidden years of Jesus than the act of sprinkling incense on charcoal. I could imagine Joseph teaching the boy Jesus about its meaning and Jesus, as a teenager, sitting on the Temple Mount, inhaling the fragrance of the resin of Saba and watching it rise, carrying the scent of praise to His Father.

The American Catholic Conference of 1978 said it clearly: "Because it is symbolic communication, liturgy is more dependent on past tradition than many human activities."[12]

Incense to me has always made the past immediate.

Still today, when it touches the senses, I hear the boy inside me whisper secret things to that God-boy in Nazareth.

But it was not just the incense, the statues, that the letter-writers hated. It was the whole picture, the very idea of placing God first.

Incense is for God-centred worship, clear and simple. And it clouds over the "spirit of the world" that permeates the people-centred worship to which Vatican II gave rise.

"We wish to continue the Sunday School practice in the basement during the homily under the guidance of Sister Eleanor."[13]

At no time in a child's life is it more important for him or her to be at a parent's side than during mass. The ploy of removing children to the basement is just one more assault on family life, one more exercise of wilfulness by those misguided, frustrated meddlers who see day-care as the answer to all the threats family life must have represented to them at one time.

The inference in this letter-writer's complaint is that children were being ignored and the services of this Sister Eleanor not appreciated.

In fact, during the Oratorians' tenure, two Sisters and a Brother conducted catechism for the flood of children who made the Oratory home on Saturday and Sunday. As Ashley explained, all was based on the three bedrock principles of the faith.

"The Apostles' Creed and the Nicene Creed are the basic summaries of the faith. Also the traditional teaching of the church is always emphasized — going through each of the Ten Commandments, so they might hear an explanation of them adopted to their age."[14]

And, nourishing the belief that every child in his soul is an artist, they taught the art of prayer. How? Simple. Father Ashley added, in terms characteristic of the approach of the Oratorians, "St. Thomas Aquinas mentioned how the 'Our Father' teaches the art of prayer."

"We want to be a part of the consultation process in

making changes that will affect us. We want to feel that
we are comfortable and our children are comfortable
with the Parish priest."[15]

"Comfortable" is the last word I would use to describe
what the children of St. Brigid's felt around the Oratorian
priests and Brothers — nothing so passive as comfort. The
children who flooded the Oratory on weekends were involved,
challenged, taught, tutored, led. They were alert, vital,
respectful, happy and gradually more and more accomplished
in the countless extensions of the liturgy that filled the weekly
programs.

"Years of careful planning for the Family liturgy
and its concomitant religious reflection programme
under the guideline of parents and senior high school
students, have gone to waste. ... There now exists a
clear discontinuity between the religious education
taught to the children at school, and that given in the
parish events."[16]

These comments reveal the writer's stunning naïvety. At
the time that this letter-writer's pretense of responsible parental
concern for Catholic education was delivered to the
Archbishop's desk, no fewer than twenty Catholic families
had withdrawn their children from the Catholic schools in his
archdiocese and undertaken the arduous and costly burden of
home-schooling in protest against the errors being taught in
his Ottawa schools.
Typical of the carefully worded misrepresentation in the
letters was:

"Participation by the congregation is limited and
uncertain."[17]

In all, at the Oratory, there were twenty-eight trained
altar boys, thirty-seven trained adults in the Gallery Choir,
twenty children in the Children's Choir, lay readers at the first
mass, rosary leaders at Our Lady's Oratory each thirteenth of

the month, six collection plate ushers, eight adult processional
assistants. Not enough? Ashley, offering an insight into why
the sanctuary of the Oratory was not regularly populated by
half a dozen expressionless ex-nuns, explained, "There is a
role reversal that seems to be taking place. The lay people are
doing everything the priests usually do and the priests are
doing what the lay people should be doing. You get a
tremendous role reversal that doesn't really express the
authentic life of the Church."[18]

The letter-writers were art critics as well. One letter
mentioned,

> "... the reappearance of numerous statues void of
> any artistic quality and diverting the attention from the
> celebration of the Eucharist as the community event of
> Christians."[19]

Of course we could hide them from view with a few acres
of felt banners with nursery school cut-outs on them. We
know the great artistic quality of those Vatican II devices. My
all-time favourite was a twelve-footer with a yellow circle of
a sun and the awe-inspiring slogan "The son is up." Son, not
sun — get it?

Talking down to an archbishop is one way of making him
wonder if you know something he does not. Example (the
following includes what is probably a quote from the Oratory):

> "Ministers of communion have been dismissed for,
> 'When there is a priest, there is no need for lay ministers,'
> even though this results in unnecessary prolongation of
> communion time."[20]

The "need for speed" factor so beloved by "People
Church" advocates is one of the distortions of Vatican II
guidelines that really unmasks these supposedly informed
letter-writers.

"Unnecessary prolongation of communion time"?

In all my years in jammed and crowded churches in the

'40s and '50, I never once heard anyone complain about the speed of communion. For sheer gratuitous interference this complaint ranks right along with the two standard reasons given for ripping out communion rails: "To increase circulation,"[21] (a curious requirement now that Vatican II has emptied half the churches) and "To give everyone unimpeded access to communion."[22]

It follows from this statement that unimpeded access to communion could only be perfected by seating twelve people at a time around the altar, for surely the writer would not consider the arrangement satisfactory to Christ to be unsatisfactory to her. Consider all the wonderful monitoring and ushering jobs such arranging would create for all those lay people with nothing to do. But might this not cause unnecessary prolongation of communion time?

> "We have lived through and supported the Vatican II changes that meet the needs of the Twentieth Century. We are adamant that we do not regress to a pre-Vatican II format."[23]

How, I wonder, have the needs of the twentieth century been met by the laicization of 50 to 60 thousand clergy? The emptying of churches? What twentieth-century need was met by those American nuns who published their kiss-and-tell diaries about lesbians behind the veil? And how do you suppose the twentieth century will survive the embarrassment of having to admit that the liberation of the countries of Eastern Europe and the annihilation of communism was led by authentic Roman Catholic churches that had remained virtually untouched by Vatican II?

Then, too, how can anyone take seriously the petulant stamping of feet of adamant Modernists who are still concerned with meeting "the needs of the twentieth century" when everyone else, from Peking to Pocatello, from Pope to Princess, is firming up lunch appointments for the twenty-first century?

When I said these people were stuck in the '60s I should have clarified it — the 1860s.

In a letter to Plourde dated December 4, 1987, the Sisterhood gave its own ninety-one-gun salute.

"We are enclosing the signatures of 91 Parishioners who request that the Oratorians leave immediately and that our territorial parish be returned to us. The 91 names on the petition so far, was [sic] signed with the promise that we commit ourselves to return to St. Brigid's."[24]

Plourde, in a blatant abuse of all principles of fairness, refused to note for his readers that the opposing petition in favour of keeping the Oratorians contained eight hundred signatures.

I wonder what St. Brigid would have thought of all this.

She is a difficult saint to interpret. A contemporary of St. Patrick, she has been the subject of as much myth-making as St. Patrick and St. Francis combined.

Her Oratory was a humble cell beneath the oak. From there, word of her virtue and sanctity spread over all Ireland so that in her own time she was known as Mary of the Gaels. She was an abbess, and among other legends is the one suggesting she may have been a bishop. She had a special compassion for the poor, and gave away all her possessions to them.[25]

She is buried in Downpatrick close by that other great oak, St. Patrick himself.

What, one must wonder, would she say to those women racing around her parish sixteen centuries later like hammerhead sharks in a feeding frenzy, claiming that St. Brigid was a practitioner of benevolent witchcraft, that she was actually a bishop, the ceremony consecrating her as an abbess being mistakenly taken from the formula for consecrating a bishop, that the symbols of her story — the oak and the eternal flame — and her knowledge of agriculture prove she was a pantheist, an animist, a druid, and heaven knows what else. The fact that her feast day is February 1, the first day of the Celtic spring, for long a pagan festival, fuels as many questions as there are people who look to St. Brigid for answers.

"The homilies are of excessive length and
concentrate on hell damnation, emphasise obligations
and confession."[26]

Priests who were strong-willed enough to reject all those
corrupting trends of the post-conciliar Catholic culture, priests
who exhibited in their dress, attitude and prayer-filled schedules
that they were not "of this world," whose devotion to the
sacraments demonstrated in no uncertain terms that Christians
were destined for a greater, fuller life than this and would only
earn it through the grace dispensed by God in accordance to
our works, were not about to strobe their audiences with the
flash, fashion and fury of a rock-video performance.

But most of all, and here we come at last to the red-hot
rivet rattling around relentlessly in the Modernist's helmet,
they instructed in that "charter of life and love," as Monsignor
Vincent Foy calls it, that is the taboo of the post-'60s church,
Humanae Vitae.

A January 7, 1988, letter offered:

"The sacrament of confession is literally shoved
down people's throats, a pervading sense of guilt is
fostered."[27]

For those not completely converted to airhead status by
Matthew Fox, the "silenced" California Dominican, promoter
of Creation Spirituality, and his claptrap about "our Original
Goodness," the acknowledgement of sinfulness and resultant
guilt remains the single most potent factor in the maturing of
consciences. How Catholics have responded to this awareness
of sin since Vatican II represents a broad spectrum of spiritual
exercise. The rationalistic, humanistic, socialistic response
simply says "The Good News is — we are the Good News."

The Oratorians' constant availability for confession
represented the traditional priestly function. The line-ups
were equally constant, drawing people from across the city
and beyond, and whenever the Oratorians served in other
parishes, their confessionals attracted similar line-ups. Clearly,
their confessional was saying something to those Catholics.

Up to this point, the contents of the *Information Bulletin* were simply condemnatory and snide, depicting the Oratorian supporters as being "of a certain vintage"[28] and the Oratorians as being disobedient. But there is one area on which all priests are vulnerable, and once libelled on those grounds can never be rehabilitated. Plourde made full use of its potential.

The issue is finance. On this, Plourde delivered his *"coup de grâce."* "Although attendance marginally increased, the parish finances have not improved."

He then proceeded to publish details of St. Brigid's ledger, as if to prove mismanagement, incompetence, irresponsibility and deceit. "How can we say a parish has been 'rejuvenated' when it is in such poor financial health?" he added.[29]

The enormity of this fantasy betrays a skilled distortion of reality.

The Oratorians had taken on a church deeply in debt, far in arrears in payment of diocesan tax, with a building falling apart, a furnace that did not work and an empty parish to draw from.

"As of May 31, 1989 they owe $80,578.23 to the Diocesan Parish loan fund," Plourde wrote.[30]

They had bought a furnace, among other things, which effectively saved the building from ruin, and as for bringing the church out of debt, they had been on the premises for less than two years!

In that time, collections multiplied, a restoration fund grew and donations to the education fund allowed them to keep four novices in university. On top of this, in a six-month period from December 1988 to May 1989, their efforts at a period restoration of St. Brigid's received commitments from three federal and provincial government ministries and departments for $510,000 to spend on the interior and for twelve months of on-the-job training for six female apprentice restorers.

I know priests whose reputation for financial acumen precedes them wherever they go. I know others who, thirty years after a financial error, are still not allowed to forget.

The lie "He's no good with money" is the assassin's

ultimate weapon, terrorism in a whisper.

For this, Plourde earned the disgust of his own priests and the scorn of Catholics at large. Everyone knew this was dirty, dirty pool. He had crossed over that border that separates what is reparable from what is not.

And now we come to the anthem of all those *Humanae Vitae* dissenters who will go to their graves insisting that God created the World in six days sometime during 1960 as a playground for their individual consciences.

> "Sensitive issues such as abortion are insensitively handled in a non-dialogue situation."[31]

I wonder what "a non-dialogue situation" means. Oh, I know — canoeing alone up the Ottawa River is a non-dialogue situation. Could that be how the Oratorians showed their insensitivity to the sensitive issue of abortion? What, now — you don't suppose the complaint refers to preaching? No doubt the complainer rejected said handling in a non-accepting way. But courteously sat through it in a non-standing sort of way. Then stomped home angrily in a non-happy sort of way. Where she spelled out her grievance in a poison pen letter to her archbishop in a non-misspelled sort of way.

The Carthaginians handled the sensitive issue of unwanted children in a decidedly non-sensitive sort of way; they threw them into a furnace alive.

They were so sensitive to the need for a God who would be agreeable to their way of doing things they went out and imported one. Is that where this comment was leading?

Up until this point in the Archbishop's listing of reasons for the Oratorians' expulsion, it was possible to suppose the whole mess was merely the result of the archdiocese of Ottawa falling into the hands of the lunatic fringe, the ignorant, the arrogant, the self-centred and self-indulgent. But the next complaint made it clear that much more was at work than simple, old-fashioned malevolence. The words strike at the very heart of Catholic worship, devotion and meditation.

They are a violent, vicious, brutal assault on the flame glowing pure and perfect at the very heart of Catholicism. They confirm nothing less than a frank denial of the Real Presence at the altar of Roman Catholic belief.

> "The excessive attention paid to the tabernacle by means of reverences, totally ignores the community event of the Eucharist itself taking place around the altar in front."[32]

In 1981, when the restoration of a Jesuit mission church was undertaken in Northern Ontario, the tabernacle was found in a ditch thirty miles away by an artist out looking for spring colour. That desecration of that empty tabernacle pales in comparison to the words of desecration contained in this savagely self-centred assault.

It does not take a rocket-scientist to read the damage done the faithful by the disorientation resulting from the shifting of the tabernacle.

Take a child's favourite toy, put it where he does not expect to see it and he will cry bitterly suspecting that someone is attempting to deceive him. Move an old man's rocking chair five inches away from where it has been for years and he will be terribly hurt from the only assumption he can make, that you are attempting to demean him in some way. Take a teenager's mirror and tack it to the back of her bedroom door so that to look at it she must become a contortionist and you will hear her fury for the hour it takes her to fix her hair. Take a heart patient's pills and put them out of reach and you will be responsible for a life.

The intention of the Vatican Council with regards to the moving of the tabernacle from its historic place of honour front and centre of the sanctuary was supposedly to fix it in a side chapel specifically arranged for adoration.

Instead, the tabernacle has been sidelined precariously on temporary podiums in far-off corners and relegated to the most humbling treatment imaginable. The abuse to which the tabernacle has been subjected since Vatican II would have sent Teresa of Avila to an early grave.

"People Church" architects have outdone themselves at designing the most hideous interiors conceivable — pews angled to face the table altar, the tabernacle set off somewhere in the gloom so that to view it you have to twist your body in direct opposition to everything the shape and angle of the pews is telling your body.

As if to compensate for the embarrassment of still having a tabernacle at all, designers have looted science-fiction magazines to come up with more and more outrageous designs. The tabernacle in the Marylake Monastery at King City, Ontario, looks like the front of an old Chevy after a five-car pile up. At St. Francis Church in Toronto, a tabernacle that looks like a gold-plated, badly dented garbage can sits on a podium like a jack-o'-lantern for kids to muse over.

If the Holy Spirit Himself should one day acknowledge that the outcome of Vatican II was in fact inspired by Him (a happening I think most unlikely), there remains one person to blame for the desecration of the sanctuary and the tabernacle in particular, and that is the priest whose church it is.

"But she will walk out if I disagree with her, one priest said when asked how he could allow the lay monsters in his Ottawa church to turn his mass into a Romper Room event. So let them walk out. Who needs them? A priest who will allow the Blessed Sacrament to be disgraced, humiliated and shuffled about week after week like a piece of annoying excess furniture should be booted out of the Catholic Church.

And any individual in archbishop's clothes who would include this appalling statement among the reasons for condemning and expelling the Oratorians should not only have no authority over Catholics, he probably is no longer even Catholic himself.

As far as the so-called collegiality of bishops is concerned, any one of those old boys from the Canadian Conference of Catholic Bishops who read that statement of insult to the tabernacle of the Blessed Sacrament and did not burn up the phone lines giving it to Plourde on both cheeks lost for himself the "soldier of Christ" ranking he received at the moment of his own confirmation slap.

When St. Charles Borromeo impressed upon the

Council of Trent the importance of moving the tabernacle front and centre of the high altar, he was finalizing fifteen hundred years of liturgical development, all of it maturing in that work of unparalleled brilliance, the Tridentine mass. The sacrifice at the centre of the Tridentine mass was the heart of Christianity; the tabernacle was the resting place of the fruit of that sacrifice. The tabernacle front and centre of the high sanctuary provided day and night, year in and year out, throughout the four hundred turbulent years since Trent, the single most powerful unifying force in Catholicism — an unequalled focus on the sacred.

Today, can anyone doubt that the Church needs, as it has never before needed in its history, unity within? Never mind ecumenical unity. How can the Catholic Church pursue unity among Christians when its own unity no longer exists? Until the sacred focus of the faith, the tabernacle, is replaced front and centre, the fragmentation of the Church will continue.

At last the Modernists have spelled it out, what they have meant all along by their demeaning of the sacred, the mishandling of sacred vessels, the abusive treatment of the hosts, the refusal to show any deference to the priest, the determination not to let slip even the faintest sign of respect for the tabernacle, the complete refusal to genuflect at the consecration, or even kneel, standing throughout as though absolutely nothing of significance was going on. In all these brutal ways they are saying welcome to "the Church of Nothing There."

It can hardly be a surprise, that in an age when the sacred is devalued as never before in history, the Church is daily being torn asunder by horrific behaviour on the part of a wilful, abusive, sexually lascivious clergy.

The scandals ricocheting through the Catholic Church will not end until the tabernacle is returned to its rightful place of honour, front and centre of every Catholic house of worship.

7

Latch-keys

A man worries about his falling hair every day for years. Then the day comes when he looks in the mirror and realizes there is nothing to worry about any more.

Amid the ever-shifting priorities of the post-conciliar Church, the man in the pew was like a pauper in Las Vegas. Sunday became a day of liturgical roulette. Those who believed it would not last, that a return to order was inevitable, sat passively while the sacraments were stolen away from them, realizing all too late that the turning point was passed. The unthinkable had crept up and overtaken them.

One day the man in the pew looked up and the Church was not there any more. Nobody was home. It was as if the Church, after years of being a constant mother, had gone off to "find herself," leaving us all latch-key kids.

On June 14, 1989, I watched, numb with sorrow, as thirty-five Canadian bishops in full regalia entered Notre Dame basilica for a celebration honouring Archbishop Plourde upon his retirement. It was just one in a seemingly endless list of commemorative events drummed up by his bureaucrats to imprint the achievements of their tenure on the public mind before they all found themselves out of work. The round of fêtes would have exhausted any bureaucrat with a normal ego, but their appetite for honours was insatiable. The orgy of flattery and praise shovelled up and over Plourde for days leading up to this farewell ceremony was well orchestrated, with the hope, no doubt, that it would be well noted by the incoming archbishop.

It is said that bishops never lose their balance — as long as they don't look down. But the little people Plourde had been ignoring for so long finally got his attention and caused him to commit a high-altitude *faux pas*.

The parishioners knew that June 14 was their last chance to make their support of the Oratory known to Plourde. The Archbishop had refused to meet with any of the throng of faithful drawn from all over the region to the Oratory. After twelve months of stonewalling, they decided to make him a visual offer he and his bishops could not refuse. They picketed his big moment, and prayed the rosary as he paraded by. The media had a field day. In an effort to condemn the demonstrators in his *Information Bulletin*, he printed the letter they handed out to those who were attending the event. His tactics backfired, because the letter spelled out their grievances succinctly and clearly. It read:

Your Grace:

We, parishioners of St. Brigid's Church, want to know why our views on the expulsion of the Oratorian Fathers are not being heard. We are given no reasons for this action and our petitions have fallen on deaf ears. Time and time again we have had the chancery door slammed in our faces. You have chosen to dismantle our parish community. We are now denied our right to worship in the legitimate manner of our choice. You clearly have no regard for us and our families.

How much longer are we expected to endure what appears to be a long trail of lies and deceit from the Ottawa Chancery? Our Oratorians are told to be silent about their plight, yet the chancery speaks openly. Non-parishioners are permitted to set up kangaroo courts in your palace to try and harangue our priests.

You, archbishop, will not even respond to our letters. Every liturgical abuse imaginable is permitted in this diocese, from altar girls to general absolution. At St. Brigid's never was a rubric violated, yet the Oratorians were a target of your chancery. This list goes on and on.

Our Oratorians were silenced, censored, slandered, harassed and finally, banished by the stroke of your pen. Where is the justice and charity for loyal and obedient Catholics? All we ask is our priests and our worship—you, Archbishop, refuse to even listen.[1]

Plourde could not resist a retort as he passed the protesters, and the words he chose proved beyond a doubt that the shepherd was not even remotely concerned with the needs of this part of his flock.

"You are only hurting your chances," he snapped.

But they knew better. It was all over long ago. It was only their sense of justice that demanded their plight be laid bare before the bishops gathered there.

First came a chorus line of thirty-some bishops, tense, uptight, as if the keys in their backs had been overwound by their secretaries.

Like their counterparts from other countries, the Canadian bishops had gone to Vatican II dreaming the dreams of greatness that are known to overtake stout, male airline passengers in mid-Atlantic, especially if they are wearing red or purple socks, destination Rome.

Did they know they were about to resolve once and for all the rancour over the Pope's infallibility that had simmered in Christendom since the First Vatican Council? The problem was merely one of exclusivity. The Bishop of Rome need not be the only one infallible. The solution was all so simple. They returned, infallible to a man, needing neither pope nor priest to puff up their ego. Secretaries, that's what they needed. And limousines. And a good, hard-working lobbyist to nominate them to civic honours. Oh yes, and of course they still needed the little people in the pews to fill the collection plates.

From that day on, the Pope needed them more than they

needed the Pope, and the Canadian bishops would spare no effort to let him know it.

But what they did not know was what every Catholic has always known, that without the Pope, without the robes, in the increasingly securalized society they were helping to bring into being, they would be nothing more than glorified office managers or, what with their "spirit of Vatican II" fantasies emptying churches everywhere — real estate entrepreneurs.

Their antics over the years had stripped the Church of its garments. However they had, of course, reserved for themselves the robes, the crook and mitre. There is something rather jaw-slackening about the sight of thirty bishops in full drag turning a corner on Sussex Drive. Many of those shuffling by had missed out on the smile-school Vatican II priests were processed through, so what the public got was a grimace and uncertain eyes, shifting glances, tight grins, giving all a furtive expression.

"What the Church needs is holiness not management," Cardinal Ratzinger says.[2]

Once in the church, the thirty bishops sat behind Plourde below the patriarchs, prophets, evangelists, fourteen doctors of the Church, sixteen founders of religious orders and nine choirs of angels.

Plourde sat on a chair throne in front of the table altar, robed and mitred with crook in hand, looking for all the world like the Atahuallapa in the last act of Peter Shaffer's *Royal Hunt of the Sun*, waiting for the sunlight to strike him and restore him to life. In the Atahuallapa's case, under the royal garments was the scar of Pizarro's garrotte, which had strangled him the day before. Under the Archbishop's robes was just a tired old man with enough qualified successors among the dignitaries assembled there to guarantee that a restoration to power, by the sunlight or otherwise, had a snowball's chance in hell of ever being realized.

I stood with my back to a pillar, having borrowed a camera to legitimize my appearance and get within scrutinizing distance of the sanctuary, from where I could see all the mitred heads.

Catholics are raised never to say an unkind word about their priests and bishops. This, of course, is something the bishops know well. It seems to me they use it extravagantly to take advantage of the faithful. With the admonition "Never criticize a bishop" burned into the Catholic's mind, bishops have been free to do what they wish, all the while being certain that the little people will continue to pay, pray and obey.

Any challenge to the bishops or criticism of how they operate is called "bishop-bashing." More than one news editor, news programmer and author has been intimidated into silence by the accusation that he is indulging in "bishop-bashing." Curiously, it has the same effect that threats of excommunication once carried. It increases the weight of the bishop's hand, gives him extra knuckles.

Once the "bishop-bashing" label has silenced troublesome editors and producers, then the Canadian bishops are free to indulge in their favourite pastime — "pope-bashing."

And so we have a Church in Canada thumbing its nose at Rome, at the Pope's declared wishes. Pandering to countless special interest groups that have created a tidal wave of challenges to the authority of the pope, they have allowed the issues of celibacy, married clergy, women in the priesthood, homosexuality and bizarre liturgy experiments to completely separate them from Rome and from the pious, determined faithful they were commanded to shepherd. It's an old boys' club thriving on the fantasy that they are more important than the Pope. One bishop even went so far as to explain laboriously in the magazine of the Catholic Women's League how the Pope is merely the Vicar of Peter while they, the bishops, are Vicars of Christ.[3]

So intimidated is this club by the feminists' innovations in the liturgy that when a woman Lutheran minister was invited to bless a Catholic High School student body with a spruce bow, the bishops fell over one another to get themselves photographed for the Catholic press doing the same.[4] Clearly the bishops of Canada are in rehearsal for "The Marx Brothers Do Rome."

Who can doubt that it is the direct fault of their bishops that lascivious neo-vampires in the guise of priests and Brothers have been permitted again and again to be reappointed to pastoral duties even after their sexual abuse of youths in their charge is well known and in various cases even verified by court convictions?

Come on boys. How stupid do you think we are? Somehow we still believe in a Church that is so flawed it could appoint flounders like you to positions of authority, but don't press your luck.

When I was fourteen and Bishop Jennings struck my cheek in confirmation to make me a "Soldier of Christ" and enlist me in defence of the faith, I never dreamed I would be defending it against bishops.

By playing the shell game with abusive, unworthy priests you have betrayed the souls in your trust. By allowing seminaries to become so corrupt that such people can actually reach ordination speaks louder than any of your public relations efforts can about the degree of negligence of which you are capable.

You have betrayed by your incompetence and arrogance those who are sorrow-laden by allowing Dignity priests in your midst to lobby for media attention and by promoting Dignity in the most scandal-ridden decade in this century's Church history.

Plourde, upon retirement, left in his wake an archdiocese that flaunts its rejection of Rome by promoting "Dignity," a support group for Catholic homosexuals that does not promote abstinence, celibacy, chastity or self-denial. This association is banned by the Vatican from using church facilities.[5] His is an archdiocese where a parish priest has appeared on television in a trendy liturgical caftan to express "astonishment" at the "lack of compassion" shown towards gays by Catholics who support Rome's ban on Dignity.

Plourde left behind an archdiocese where a Dignity conference welcomed and applauded Father John McNeill, a Jesuit expelled from his order for his promotion of same-sex activity in such statements as "The love which unites the partners, rather than alienating them from God can be judged as uniting them more closely with God and as mediating God's presence in our world."[6]

McNeill denies the authority or credibility of the Church's

"Pastoral Care of Homosexual Persons" on the grounds that it is homophobic!"[7] For this, McNeill was applauded in Ottawa by many of that recurring cast of characters who mounted the anti-Oratorian campaign, dominate the staff of the local school of Thigh-ology and recently gave a foot-stomping, cheering ovation to Matthew Fox on his recent descent into Ottawa whenever he punctuated his "Original Goodness" manifesto with tirades against Rome.

The Ottawa scenario is depressingly familiar – a small clique of Dignity priests and theologians projecting the tiresome attitude that everybody in the world is gay, they just don't know it. The result is that students and seminarians have to deal face-to-face with overt homosexuality that, once just the meat of anti-Catholic jokes, is now all too tragically a reality.

Ever anxious to make use of any lever to unbalance the Church's stand on a celibate clergy, these same priests and theologians point with exclamations of "Aha!" to the Mount Cashel Orphanage and other boarding schools, where a rampage of sexual abusers have brought an indelible scandal on the Church. As if a network of criminal pedophiles would care about celibacy rules! In wake of the Mount Cashel scandal, Chesteron's "halo of hatred around the Church of God" was fairly glowing and throbbing, nowhere brighter than in Ottawa, where the gleeful clique of Dignity advocates had free reign to use the scandal to further justify their existence. This is the result, they argue, of the "unnatural suppression of sexual instincts."

This, of course, is simple craziness. At a time when the entire world is seized by the horrible fall-out from the sexual revolution, Dignity priests and theologians are encouraging gay Catholics to come out of the closet, socialize under the church roof and pursue their sexual orientation. How did such an embarrassing state of affairs come about in Ottawa? In the same way that Mount Cashel came about in St. John's. Pedophiles congregated in Mount Cashel for the same reason that Dignity priests and nuns gravitated to Ottawa — because they knew they could.

If ever there was a time for the clergy to preach restraint and responsibility it is now. Now is the hour in Church history for the principles of "Courage" to be promoted. "Courage" is the Church's alternative to the Dignity agenda, and it is currently taking root across North America. It represents a unique undertaking in which non-heterosexuals form support groups for the purpose of strengthening their resolve to pursue celibacy and chastity. "Courage" employs the famous "Twelve Steps" as its backbone, a formula for self-examination that has assisted millions who wanted to break their reliance on alcohol, drugs and other dependencies. Courage is also finding it is being mirrored by like programs in other denominations. The heart and soul and strength of the Courage program is prayer. Through the rosary and sacraments, the individual, with group support, rediscovers the true meaning of the term "dignity."

As he piloted his unsinkable ego toward retirement, Plourde resembled not King Arthur going to his well-earned rest but the captain of the *Titanic*, blithely sailing westward, eyes fixed on the horizon for signs of glory, while a great lavender iceberg sodomized steerage. And the band played on.

You, bishop, have betrayed the good and saintly nuns who have determined to live out their vows in obedience to the Church when you permit ex-nun would-be-women-priests to conduct imitation witchcraft rituals in diocesan facilities. This is not diversity. This is demonic games playing.

You have betrayed the children of the Church, who in Catholic schools no longer learn of "the Virgin who shall conceive," the Trinity, the virtues of faith, hope and charity, the laws of the Church, the lives of the saints. This is not diversity. This is the scandalizing of youth.

You have broken your promise. You have reneged on your commitment. You have left the faithful with one certainty: that it need never bother looking to you to justify the Roman Catholic faith in this country unless you are cornered, or unless it has some media advantage.

Do you bishops not realize that you are finished? That the only class of religious more despised in this country after sex-offenders, published lesbian ex-nuns and ex-priests playing in gay piano bars are you good old boys who let it happen, pretended you did not know, or were out of town on business? Who is going to clean up the mess you have left behind after you have all had your dinners of tribute and grandstand retirement shows?

You are what is wrong with Roman Catholicism in Canada. You are bad managers, guys. You can order councils and committees and seminars and workshops until the cows come home but you cannot escape Pope John Paul II's simple prescription: " The Church of today does not need any new reformers. The Church needs new saints" (*The Ratzinger Report*).

Looking at these impassive, inexpressive faces of those bishops ranged in rows around the sanctuary, the individual could easily conclude that other old adage to be true, that "when a priest becomes a bishop he gets the face that he deserves."

One might then suppose that the only hope for the Church in Canada is that St. Teresa of the Little Flower was word-perfect when quoting her Père Pichon, who said, "Souls differ more than faces."[8]

The picture presented to the public on this sad occasion was one of politics, power, vanity, a frenzy of self-promotion and a fetish for rich menus. Those bloated, puffed-up ego balloons arrayed in the sanctuary, if polled, would, to a man, plead 300 percent support for all that Vatican II stands for, which, if you recall Pope John XXIII's words, was intended "to return the Church to the simple form it had when it left the hand of Jesus Christ, its founder."

Had Jesus walked in the door of Notre Dame that day, He no doubt would have been approached and whispered to harshly about His inappropriate attire, lack of style, bad timing, and asked to step back out of the way.

We all know what His reaction would be. He would make a whip of knotted cords and drive that curious collection of personalities fleeing into the traffic of Sussex Avenue with their crooks and mitres. The honouree, Plourde, would no doubt have thought this out of keeping with "the most elementary principles of Christian charity."

We all dream, at send-offs like this one, that one speaker at least will get up and tell the truth. But the address was given by Governor-General Jeanne Sauvé. At least she had the honesty to dress and act in keeping with the totally overblown artificiality of the whole affair. She sat in the front pew in a pastel suit, her expression not visible under a large, deep-brimmed hat that consumed most of her head.

In her fawning address, she recited Plourde's achievements, noting that in the archdiocese of Ottawa the mass was said in twenty-six languages. She did not mention that Latin, the language of the Church for seventeen centuries, was available only on the edge of the city, where Plourde had exiled the Tridentine mass to a former Jehovah's Witness Hall for anyone who could afford a car to drive that far. Latin in the fast lane.

The pickets on the sidewalk stole the day. The media dealt with their display in all four colours. The bishop was barely in the picture.

Plourde's fury came spilling out in the *Information Bulletin*:

> These priests and their supporters seem to think that they know better than the bishop.[9]

This was followed, of course, by his usual refrain on "basic Christian charity."

At the end of this *Information Bulletin*, the hand that wrote it permitted itself to ask a few questions under the guise of an archbishop talking to himself.

> "What would become of a Church where each pastor took the same individualistic approach as they [the Oratorians] have?"[10]

Plourde had only to look across the length and breadth of his archdiocese for the answer to that one. Experimental liturgies, improvised lay involvement and outrageous tampering with the canon of the mass were the rule, not the exception.

"Without the bishop's direction, what would happen to the unity which is indispensable for proclaiming Christ our Saviour?"[11]

Unity? With a bishop's direction?

It was inevitable that what the Oratorians brought to Lowertown would gradually change Lowertown itself. Within blocks of the famous Byward Market and the community of art schools, galleries, clubs and shops surrounding it, the Oratorians were providing added justification for the arts crowd to take up residence there. It was customary to see young musicians sitting in the rear pews beating out rhythms on their knees, or a writer sketching notes and photographers gauging the light. What the Oratorians brought to Lowertown was artistic life, with all its precious diversity on display.

What a legacy Archbishop Plourde would have left behind had he been able to withstand the prejudices and pressures of the times.

8

Eviction

The terse reply from Cardinal Innocenti to the Petition for Recourse submitted by the Oratorians ended all wishful thinking. Dated May 12, 1989, it declared: "... that recourse cannot be accepted by this Dicastery. None of your rights have been violated by the action of the Archbishop."[1]

What about the rights of the faithful who flocked to the Oratory?

Father Ashley, wistful and philosophical upon accepting the finality of it, commented:

"For us, of course, another very fundamental point is the whole idea of religious freedom. There was tremendous emphasis at Vatican II on religious freedom.

"That's why I can't understand that attitude. I mean, surely to goodness people are free to worship God in the mould that they find most adapted to themselves within the Catholic Church according to the authentic norms that the Church gives to us.

"We were not violating any of those norms. We were working within the parameters that the Church provides for us. So I can't understand how you can have all of this talk about religious freedom, all this talk about pluralism and diversity and not put up with different ways of doing things.

"Why should these faithful be treated as second-class citizens in the Church, especially when the Pope has said that they have a right to have these things. We should be providing these things for people who want them."

And they did want them. Ashley recalled the numbers that confirmed the point.

"I remember my first Saturday evening mass. I was at the back of the church, and the previous pastor was with me. I put on the vestments and looked out at the church. I looked at my watch. It was five o'clock. I turned to him and said, 'I guess the people are coming?' and he said, 'This is it.' You could have fired a cannonball through the church and it wouldn't have hit anybody.

"There has been tremendous increase in attendance, there's no doubt about that. At the nine o'clock mass, one parishioner told me his son used to count on his hands twice over to come up with the number of people in the church. Now it's up to approximately 150. The Sunday mass at eleven would have about 100. That's all I could ever remember seeing there. Now there are an average of 325. It was quite a big embarrassment to the Modernists in the archdiocese, like many a bureaucracy that becomes totally out of touch with people they're supposed to be serving. It is typical of 'intellectualoids' to think that they know the mind of the people, to be always talking for the people but never really realizing....

"For example, we had a petition given to us signed by almost seven hundred people asking for a regular celebration of the Latin mass when we were still in the archdiocese of Vancouver.

"Well, of course, that is a tremendous embarrassment because what they think of as an outdated mentality, something all finished with, was not finished at all. The new image that they wanted to give to the Church had not taken root in the minds and hearts of all the people. It was a rude awakening to find that many people aren't satisfied with the direction things are going."

In spite of the personal hardship and private grief the Oratorians suffered when the axe finally fell, Father Ashley — boxes, trunks and suitcases daily piling higher and higher, the evidence of the Oratory's demise all around him — remained focused on the bigger issue.

"Some people accuse me of being an unconquerable optimist, saying that the future is bright. But it's only because the Church has an unconquerable life principle. The Holy Spirit is a supernatural organism. The Church has a constitution given to her by Christ himself, therefore, in that sense, it is unconquerable.

"She has known her low moments when the moral life of the faithful and the clergy tended to go for a downslide. Just the same, she also reforms herself. Slowly. But surely.

"People say, 'How come there aren't any saints today?' Well, of course, we won't know that for another hundred years. It could well be there is a whole flock of saints right here in the Church in the present moment and will be recognized as such, in time, when the Church realizes there were these saintly individuals who helped people remain faithful to the Catholic way of life.

"Sometimes it can appear that the local churches are further away from Rome than in point of fact they are.

"In the early Church, when there was a denial of the divinity of Christ, it was the lay people who maintained the faith. You could go to many churches today and say it doesn't look like there is much left, but in point of fact, the lay people do still believe. There is lots of faith.

"So we can't judge merely by appearances, although there are tremendous problems, no doubt about that. Yet, if we look deeper down we find that faith, hope and charity are still surviving in the lives of many members of the Church. There is still a tremendous amount of holiness there. That's the power of God himself. He is the giver of gifts.

"A tremendous mistake has been made in the Church. We lay so much emphasis on coming up with programs, training sessions, renewals, that we forget that what calls from the inside, the interior life, is God Himself, at work in the interior of each individual soul.

"To think that somehow or other you could reform the Church from the outside merely by coming up with new structures and new ways of doing things! It's ridiculous!...

"The church is an organic reality, has a divine life principle — God Himself. She automatically forms herself. She automatically gives people a life of grace. Those things are just there.

"You can change and play with structures all you want, but the important thing to ask ourselves is, 'Are people becoming better?'"[2]

In the final days leading up to their eviction, when there were still those who hoped that by some miracle Plourde would come to his senses, Father Ashley expressed how the Oratorians would react were the expulsion to occur.

"We will be very sad. I'm sure in a sense we'd almost shed a few tears over it. There is the supernatural side of the good we believe we've been able to accomplish. But also, on the human level too, there's all that friendship. All the people we have grown to know and love and who also have grown to know and love us. There is certainly great suffering when you have to be separated from people you have grown to know and love. They say that is one of the most bitter sufferings you can endure in life.

"If God asks it of us, of course that is what we have to do. There is no doubt we will suffer. I don't think I could say, on the other hand, there will be any bitterness. We've tried to see the thing in the perspective of eternity and say, well, it doesn't make sense to us, we can't see why this has to happen. But there must be some reason in the mind of God, even if it is just his permissive will that he allows it to happen, although we might prefer that things had gone in another direction. But no doubt, as I've mentioned, the main point is that there is a tremendous loss for us.

"The Pope says every city has a soul just like we have souls. You grow to love a city, to love the people, to become part of it, part of the whole city family. It's a tremendous loss to us to have to say goodbye to, not just the diocese, not just the church, but also to the city which we've done our best to become part of. It will be a great sadness for us to have to leave all of that."[3]

The Oratorians' inspiration and founding father, St. Philip Neri, had been desirous of joining Francis Xavier in the missions to India, but a Cistercian monk, his spiritual director, told him Rome would be his India.

Philip persevered in the capital of Christendom, earning the label "The Apostle of Rome." When he was canonized in 1622, alongside him, being elevated to the altar of the Church at the same moment, was St. Francis Xavier, "The Apostle of India."[4]

The priests and Brothers of the Oratory left St. Brigid's not as a group but as individual priests and Brothers to pursue their personal vocations in an anonymity that must have been a blessed relief after twenty-four months in the spotlight. The destiny of only one of them will be mentioned here.

Father Donald J. Neilson died on February 10, 1991, while serving the parish of Powell River, British Columbia. At the time of his sudden and unexpected death, the delightful, cultured, cordial, witty and good-humoured man who explained to me all about shadows was fifty years of age.

His death came nine days after the Feast of St. Brigid of Ireland. Nine days — one complete novena into Celtic Spring.

Part IV

Thieves at The Altar

1

Vatican Valkyries

It was a pride in all things Irish that made the late-Victorian builders of St. Brigid's push the walls higher and higher to raise a steeple that would be taller than the bishop's at Notre Dame.

Their ambitions stood proud for fourscore and ten years, at which time it was discovered that the eastern wall at the top was fourteen inches out of alignment. The shift was a reaction of the wall to the earth, which was itself reacting to the drying-up of a creek bed nearby. Around the time the Second Vatican Council was opening, St. Brigid's church was threatening to open as well, unfold, lotus-like, with a great limestone thud. A combination of exterior concrete buttresses and cables in the attic saved it from collapse.

From the choir level, steps lead through a ceiling trap door to the east tower. That ceiling in turn floors a square tower chamber two storeys high walled with grey Ottawa limestone, the "white brick" seen all over the city and deplored by Oscar Wilde in his 1881 tour of Ottawa. This bare stone keep soars upward, with steep wooden steps laddered against one wall. High overhead planks at odd angles testify to the removal of the bell, which, in a transaction conducted by the same priest who went mad with grey paint, was reputedly sold to a church in Gatineau.

Entering the attic one sees a marvellous sight. Unlike so many vault fans decorating the high naves of North American gothic structures, St. Brigid's do not push flush up against a solid vault ceiling. These vault fans open into the attic itself, so that walking the length of the attic requires tiptoeing on planks balanced between hollow fans opening to the left and the right, like giant, empty ice-cream cones.

The fourteen-inch alignment flaw that developed in the '60s was just the latest in the problems that have plagued this uppermost level of the church. In 1888, the builder, his hands locked shut on a hoisting cable, shot from the earth to the bell tower, where his hands were permanently mangled in a service pulley suspended from the church façade. Later, the crushed-paper insulation flooring the attic began filtering through ceiling cracks and into the eighty-five-year-old Cassavante organ.

But that was all over now. The Oratorians, after updating the attic wiring, had installed new lights for the ceiling of the high vault below our feet and umbrellaed the organ pipes until they could replace the ancient insulation dust. After reminding me not to step off the planks and therefore through the vault ceiling and into eternity, my guide related how at Vespers the previous Sunday evening a bat had entered the sanctuary from a hole near the altar and he had chased it around the sanctuary with a wine bottle. He told me to tread softly and slowly and pointed upward.

There they were, clumps of black in the already dark crevices, nooks and angles of the roof. Bats. Dozens, hundreds ... an infestation. Just overhead.

Here perhaps was what really had become of the dinosaurs.

Was this that same endangered species I had spied on along the hydro line back on the Madawaska in the forties? Those coiffed and veiled, black-and-white berry-pickers? No, not the beautiful Sisters of St. Joseph of my childhood. They would have taken to the trees and become swallows.

These things clinging to the darkness and the ceiling were not feathers and fluff but leather and fur, with nostrils that took up half the face. It was a mean-looking *cursillo* of hairy-backed Valkyries doing what their nature compelled them to do — experience the world upside-down all day, except for when, in deference to the laws of gravity, they would turn right-side-up to evacuate their entrails. I have little patience with bats. They may very well be harmless, as people say. And yes, it's true, they have persisted in occupying space in church structures since long before it was safe for Christians to ring bells. But just because they will not go away does not mean I should surrender my pew and missal to them, nor hang upside-down from their rafter to see things their way.

One must wonder why bats, like the Modernists, are content to usurp church space rather than evolve the skills to build their own structures. This suggests a subtlety of purpose I would not have accredited to bats, an awareness that it is necessary for them to remain in close proximity to other users of the structure in order that they may gradually transform the collective conscience — that is, get everyone turned upside-down.

Expelling the Oratorians from Ottawa differed little from throwing the tabernacle out into the ditch. It was all part of the same mind-set that had replaced Bach, Mozart and Palestrina with a five-string guitar. The Oratorians had mastery over the magisterium they taught, the music they cultivated, the art and architecture they restored.

They delivered from their pulpits homilies that upheld the magisterium, reinforced the truth that the Church is, first of all, Christ's Church, and it becomes ours only by our keeping God's law. What they offered from the pulpit was leadership, a near-extinct quality in a Church drowning in the flatulent blather spewed out weekly in Father Feelgood's Smile and Clap Emporium.

And whereas it was their supposed challenge to his authority that Plourde cited as reason for their unsuitability and the cause of division in his archdiocese, in reality it was the Oratorians' intellectual and moral grip on what they were doing that determined among the iconoclasts, feminists and left-wingers that they had to go. The liberal left cannot tolerate for even a moment any authority but its own. Had Plourde not been so easy to manipulate, they would have driven him from office. They, the left, always progress through their power ritual in the same three stages: 1. they assert that they and only they are right; 2. they enact their carnival routine of reactions — a fixed repertoire of facial and verbal performances all geared to exhibit astonishment that anyone would challenge them, then 3. they proceed to belittle, isolate, exile and ultimately annihilate the challengers.

Their most common and most effective lie is that Vatican II completely severed the Church from the past, that the break with all that came before was total and irreversible. They impress all of that upon those who are in thrall to the aura of power they exude. Anyone who exhibits piety of any sort, especially if it is recognized as having existed before 1960, is said to be part of that "outdated spirituality."

This is meant to perpetuate the myth that Modernists are on the cutting edge, the front line, riding shotgun on philosophy, theology and science to make sure it reaches the twenty-first century on time.

They would naturally exhibit great astonishment if you suggested their ideas and methods were not new. Immediately they would shut off the conversation, in case you mentioned their nemesis, Pius X, who had them all figured out in 1907.

Imagine, then, into what degrees of apoplexy they would be hurled by hearing that another pontiff had described them to the letter centuries earlier in 1223. To such theologians of his time Gregory IX wrote: "Some among you, inflated like bladders with the spirit of vanity, strive by profane novelties to cross the boundaries fixed by the Fathers."[1]

Gregory might very well have been taking his cues from an even earlier date, 787, and the Second Council of Nicea, formed to combat the Iconoclastic Heresy. That council "condemns those who dare, after the impious fashion of heretics, to deride the ecclesiastical traditions, to invent novelties of some kind or endeavour by malice or craft to overthrow any one of the legitimate traditions of the Catholic Church."[2]

Whenever they have reared their self-concerned little

heads they were recognized. In 1834 Gregory XVI noted, "A lamentable spectacle is that presented by the aberrations of human reason when it yields to the spirit of novelty...."[3]

Pius IX, no slouch when it came to recognizing anti-Church propaganda, unmasked a few glorifiers of secular humanism in 1846 with, "These enemies of divine revelation extol human progress to the skies and with rash and sacrilegious daring would have it introduced into the Catholic religion as if this religion were not the work of God but of man...."[4]

To the brilliant and astute Leo XIII, the promoters of the tiresome new world philosophy were totally transparent: "To bring contempt and odium on the mystic spouse of Christ ... the children of darkness have been wont to cast in her face a stupid calumny ... to depict her as the enemy of light, science and progress."[5]

Leo XIII in 1902 summed up the Modernists' style: "It is impossible to approve in Catholics of a style inspired by unsound novelty which seems to deride the piety of the faithful and dwells on the introduction of a new order of Christian life, on new directions of the Church, on new aspirations of the modern soul, on a new vocation of the clergy and on a new Christian civilization."[6]

Of those theologians and religious whose style is itemized above, Pius X wrote: "For them the recklessness of a writer is in direct proportion to the recklessness of his attacks on antiquity, and of his efforts to undermine Tradition and the ecclesiastic magisterium."[7]

For pointing out these guardians of the faith who have ear-tagged the Modernist manifesto whenever it appeared I am grateful to the Modernists' nemesis, Pius X, who called them by name in 1907.

The blows struck with relentless vigour at the Church by the rebel religious in this era have no parallel in history and make all other attacks on the Church throughout history seem like a mere Mad Hatter's tea party. In one generation, the Catholic Church became as helpless and lifeless as Christ abandoned on the cross, where anybody who wished could walk up and drive in a spear. The ordained and consecrated for two millennia had died at the foot of the cross defending His honour. Now, they turned on Him.

How did it happen? How did the Roman Catholic Church, the longest lasting human institution in recorded history, get itself into such a black-and-blue mess?

To fully comprehend the sorrow afflicting the Church today, one would have to have lived the last thirty years a thousand times, for the reasons are legion; I lived through it only once. Yet, of course, this sorrow has only one source, and it is rooted in the most destructive force imaginable — the illusion of liberty.

It is as if the Revolution, like a pebble thrown from the shores of time, had skipped over the waters of history touching down in Paris in 1789, in Moscow in 1917, in Peking in 1948 and then finally settled into the surf with a subtle splash in Rome some time between 1962 and 1965.

What history would record was that under Pope Paul VI at least 35,000 clergy were laicized.[8] Not all the purges in history had so devastated the Church. In the most persecution-free, liberated age in history, the priests had just walked away.

How could they have forgotten so much? Had they not, sometime in their youth, prostrated themselves before God and submitted all to Him? Were they not the Chosen, safely on solid, dry earth because God, to have them near Him, turned the sea into a sidewalk?

Had they forgotten those nights before the seminary when they lay in bed and watched with full hearts as, in the shadows overhead, God made the mountains skip like rams, the hills like lambs of the flock?

Did they not lie down before Him in submission because He had turned rocks into pools of water? And when they arose, did they not truly believe that they had, as of that moment, the power to do what was even greater, the power to forgive sin, to absolve and dissolve it, to banish it and forget it?

They had ears — did they hear not? Eyes — did they see not? Minds — did they know not? They had memories. Do they not remember?

2

Thieves

"For those who believe in Christ ... are finally established as, 'a chosen race', a royal priesthood...."[1]

In case Plourde's readers failed to detect the agenda his petitioners were selling, they finally spelled it out.

So, at last, we have come to the issue of women priests. Did anyone doubt that we would?

In 1988 Archbishop Plourde founded the Ottawa Diocesan Committee "Women in the Church." It includes on its executive some of the same individuals who initiated and propelled the campaign to oust the Oratorians and co-ordinate the letters of petition to Plourde.

The "'chosen' ... royal priesthood" quoted above is a staple phrase of women's spirituality seminars. The attraction this phrase has for dissident nuns and ex-nuns has fuelled their participation in endless workshops on feminist spirituality.

Ostensibly convened to represent Catholic women and to define more participatory roles for women in the existing Church, the workshops are actually a weaning process, aimed at breaking spiritual dependency on the existing Church and creating a new one, a matriarchal hierarchy. These workshops equate to prayers at the foot of the altar of "Women Church."

The workshops all aim at "empowerment," which, all red herrings aside, simply means building the determination to take power. "Sensitivity" is a key word in all workshops.

Interpersonal sensitivity workshops include standing face to face with another person and staring unblinking into their eyes for as long as it takes to suppress the suspicion that this is a stupid idea.

Flashback workshops include closing your eyes and regressing to your childhood to recall hurtful or joyful times. One nun in Ontario has a mandate from her enthusiastic bishop to subject gatherings of priests to this Romper Room play.

Dressing up is a step workshops eventually reach. Clowns apparently have exerted a great influence on the religious since Vatican II. Certain priests and nuns who treat the Church as if it were a circus see no contradiction in assuming Bozo noses and face markings when a clown costume is dropped in their midst.

"Nesting" is a favourite workshop of novices in feminist spirituality. The novice becomes a "stick" and some invisible bird fits her in and around other "sticks" until they are all touching and entwined and therapeutically in touch with another. They stay that way until they overcome the certainty that if parents caught children doing this they would spank them and send them home.

Sculpting workshops are very popular as well. All the participants isolate themselves on the floor, then, having communed with their inner architectural selves, they float up and together design with their assembled body parts what a church really should be.

Poetry workshops are the spring from which flows the liturgy of "Women Church." Individuals who once sought the anonymity of the veil are now reading out their innermost yearnings about the other fast-beating hearts in the room. And, of course, it is eternally fashionable to workshop the environment, on everything from the hole in the ozone to toadstools.

All of this near-incomprehensible silliness is neither surprising nor new. I said it before and I'll say it again: this is role-playing-in-the-round sensitivity workshopping straight out of the experimental theatre of the '60s. It is all familiar stuff to anyone who has partaken of even one actor's workshop.

If it was the motive of the movers and shakers of these undertakings to develop feminist theatre, to break through the barriers to people like me who sincerely want to be able to understand more of the feminists' viewpoints, aspirations and challenges, I would be the first to applaud.

But that is not at all the case. This program does not care one whit if anyone ever understands it, except the participants. Nor do they care to have anyone scrutinize them too closely.

Recently, a group of traditional Catholics who registered for a feminine spirituality workshop were told by workshop organizers, using anonymous phone calls, not to attend. When the registrants insisted on attending, the feminist organizers put on a display of power. The registrants arrived at the site of the event, the archdiocesan centre no less, to encounter three police cars and policemen barring their entry. The workshopping, role-playing-in-the-round, sharing, caring "being persons" had called in the troops.

The organizers claimed they had the Bishop's approval for this action. The bishop in question denied it. But the deed was done. The police had been manipulated into playing the first male acolytes at "Women Church." Empowerment workshops are not about education, they are about power, the way Girl Guide exercises were not about learning, they were about badges.

"Women Church," on its way to supplanting Christ's Church, may even give badges for all I know. One badge for willow-whipping a priest into letting you give a feminist homily. Another for coercing him into letting you gesture with him and touch the offerings at consecration. Another for convincing him to use brownies instead of communion wafers. Yet another for choreographing into your dance liturgy a row of waving and gesticulating nuns without making them look like escapees from a semaphore class for the senile.

"To return the Church to the simple form it had when it left the hand of Jesus Christ, its founder."

It has been a long leap from that innocent wish of John XXIII to the sight of a priestess in the presider's chair. But Rome was not dismantled in a day.

When Teilhard de Chardin penned "The Essential

Feminine" was he thinking of Mary, as he hinted, or had he just done lunch with feminist students from Anima 101? Did he suspect he could be midwifing an upside-down, inside-out surrogate Creator who would be called She, Our Mother who art in heaven? Drunk on the sap of self, today's would-be priestesses scour the Testaments, Old and New, for "royal priesthood" phrases that prophesy their arrival as the arbiters of God. But what God? The God who would paint Christ as short-sighted for being born a man? The God who would shake his head in bewilderment at Christ choosing twelve men instead of twelve women, or choosing not to select a rep-by-pop balance of six of each? Will those revisionists, after correcting the narrow choices Christ made, stop after they have escorted the Three Wise Women to the manger? Naturally not. Such consummate meddlers would unwrap the swaddling clothes to reveal that the offspring of God, the saviour of all womankind, was none other than His Only Daughter Our Championess. Then, after Adam has eaten the Apple and tempted Eve into sin, they will get down to the truth of who it really was who created the world in six days of cut-and-paste. Then at last the one instrument of teaching allowed in Her Church on earth, the felt banner, will finally tell it like it is.

Why is Mary so invisible in the Gospel? Because she was not the story. Decrease. Increase.

How will it read when rewritten by the "People Church" scribes? Why does the nouveau Church feminist edit herself in? Because she thinks she is the story.

Was it Mary who, from a distance, viewed the Agony in the Garden and supplied the writers of the gospels with the details of that Thursday night in Gethsemene? How will it be rewritten?

Was Mary interviewed by Luke to learn the details of the scene at the manger? Of the shepherds? Of the angels and the Wise Men?

When the Bethlehem story is rewritten, will the shepherds report that first they saw a stout, badly dressed, frizzy-haired woman in the sky barking out, "Now we will sing a hymn," and then there came a choir of angels?

How in the rewriting will be explained the slaughter of

the innocents? Suddenly the proportion of girls to boys in Bethlehem was altered?

How will the circumcision be rewritten? How will the sacrifice of Calvary begin? Will a dour-faced, tight-lipped sharing, caring, "being person" stop proceedings while she makes a long, solitary walk up the hill to turn her blank eyes on the multitude and bark out "Communion Antiphon ..."?

How will the Resurrection be rewritten?

And it will be. All of it. And the Church will be translated. Why does the feminist edit herself in? Into the priesthood? Because to herself and other feminists, she is what is important. Increase.

Try as they might, however, the campfire girls will never transform their club into a Church, for the purpose of their camp's existence is now and always has been a drive for power. Nothing more; nothing less. It has nothing to do with God. Nothing at all. They bought the Big Lie that said that if they pushed long enough they would ultimately find an absolute, a certainty, not in God, but in themselves. And that is why they will fail, because being the centre of the universe is never easy. Eve apparently bought the same lie, but at least she got lunch.

They are not without male support. The priests who pander to them are easily recognizable. They have turned their parish churches into chatty little boutiques where smiles and handshakes substitute for sacraments and prayer. They would rather talk about their tan, just brought back from Aruba, than catechism. They wear tight jeans and trendy T-shirts and just love it when the women fuss over their latest protégé and suggest he would make a fine deacon. They are all working on some university course vaguely related to social work and often go faint with pleasure at the sound of names like Nicaragua, El Salvador, etc. Their conversations, when not focused on the credits they are racking up for themselves in government-subsidized soup kitchens or battered women's shelters, have an awesome lifelessness about them, like stale smoke from the '60s. I suspect, had they been on the Via Dolorosa, they would have been running guns for Barabbas.

Their homilies often open with something like, "Let's

have a big hand for Deacon Rick who is just off for a trip to El
Salvador. And here's a surprise for you Rick, a going-away
present from the post-grad workers at Battered Wives —
luggage! Let's have a big hand for Rick."

I no longer bother talking to any of the Club Med
Fathers. My last conversation was enough. It happened that
I was in a local rectory awaiting one when his deacon, in the
usual Club-Med attire of jeans, T-shirt and new Adidas,
looking for all the world like his mother had been scared by a
Boy Scout, came gliding down the banister.

I wondered aloud whether or not he had caught the
"deacon's-knees disease" which seems to prevent them from
genuflecting in front of the tabernacle or at the consecration.
When I asked him why he never offered any deference on the
altar to the Real Presence, he lifted his Walkman earphone off
one ear and barked out over the music, "What present?
Where?"

Recently, in a small Ontario church, at the moment of the
elevation of the host, a whining yet brassy voice that had been
caterwauling from the choir loft all through mass every inane
piece of drivel imaginable from the latest Glory and Praise
edition began belting out "For me, for me, for me ..." It took
some moments to realize that she was singing the ending to the
Broadway song "Everything's Coming Up Roses" that Ethel
Merman chiselled into history on the stage and Rosalind
Russell enlivened in the film *Gypsy*.

I knew then that things soon had to change, for the abuse
of the liturgy could not go much further than that.

Oh, mind you, I have seen other horrors. I've seen the
Club Med Fathers drop the host on the floor then look down at
it with astonishment and bother. We've all heard of hosts
being found in the pew after mass was out. But have you met
a seminarian two years away from ordination who did not
know the words to the Hail Mary? I did. In Toronto in 1980.

He was one of those extravagant personalities who
deliver stand-up comedy routines ridiculing Mother Theresa
upon request at parties. He boasted openly that he would wear
a woman's garter-belt under his robes on ordination day to
win a bet with those friends who were to be his invited family

at the event. He was chased from St. Augustine's with quite a few others when Cardinal Carter purged it of its notorious mafia a few years later.

Of course the Oratorians had to go. They represented the conserving force of the Church, transmitting facts and dogmas, revealed truths of faith and morals, handing down the mould of the key to the kingdom that Roman Catholicism has been preserving and guarding for two millennia. Their crime was traditionalism, born of orthodoxy, executed with conversatism.

For the uninitiated to whom these terms still represent the Churchillian "riddle wrapped in a mystery inside an enigma," let me offer some word association that will help you visualize their offence.

An "orthodox" priest does not encourage mini-skirted nuns in "orthopaedic booties" to lead their liturgical dance class in arm-swinging leaps before the tabernacle.

A "traditional" priest trades contrition for sanctifying grace, renewing his faithful sacramentally from the tabernacle.

A "conservative" priest is, you guessed it, a conservationist, protecting the dry timber of his flock from the flame that never dies by sprinkling them with the Blood of the Lamb, and by teaching the survival strategies inherent in the commandments forged at the Bush that would not Burn and alloyed by the magisterium of the Church. He does this because he believes with all his heart he was commissioned to do so by the Son of God, truly real and truly present, body and blood, soul and divinity, in the tabernacle of the Roman Catholic Church.

And what of the philosophers, theologians, historians, critics and reformers, either religious or ex-religious, masculine and feminine, who conspired to remove these Traditionalists, who conspire still to ensure the Church in Ottawa today is rebuilt on their own designs?

They are thieves. The gay mafia currently infesting Ottawa's seminaries are thieves. The Dignity advocates who are hi-jacking St. Joseph's parish are thieves. The fem-agenda nuns who are clomp-clomping through the halls of power in the archdiocese sowing their agenda are thieves. The priests who ridicule parishioners praying the rosary to Mary are thieves. All of them thieves, just as surely as the thief who stole the tabernacle and threw it into a ditch thirty miles away, for they have burglarized Roman Catholicism from within, vandalized its true meaning, removed its essence from the liturgy and in its place left nothing of value. The burglars had been in the house all along.

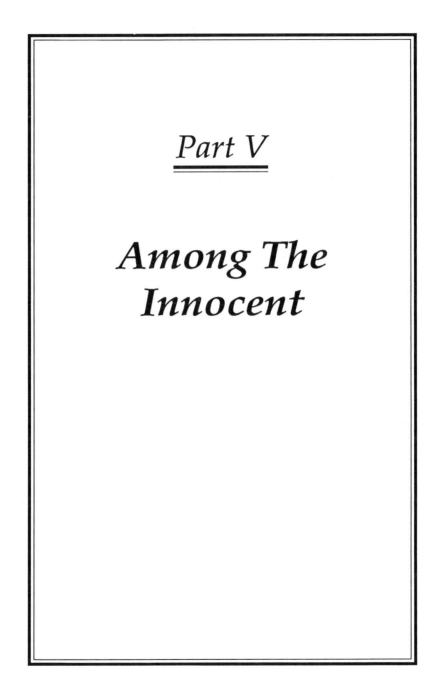

Part V

Among The Innocent

1

Corridors

Childhood is a magic room we all live in for a time and then, of course, must flee. Forever after, knowingly or unknowingly, we stalk our allotted corridors trying each and every door for one that will swing inward and let us glimpse what it is we left behind.

Is that why I tried the door of the Ottawa Oratory that fateful day in July 1988? Was it nostalgia?

Of course not. What it is we leave behind those doors leading from childhood is truth, truth as revealed to us in our infancy: truth about love or hate, depending on our parents; truth about joy and sorrow, depending on our faith; truth about pain or gain, depending on our state; truth about war and peace, depending on our family. And truth about God, depending on all of the above, and especially the truth about life and death, depending on how the story of the Son of God is imparted to us.

I went to the door of the Oratory that day because, in my childhood, I was told how, had I walked into that winding, climbing street in old Jerusalem two millennia ago, I would have seen a man, collapsed on the pavement, so beaten, so exhausted, so tortured that the blood of his body mixed with the sand of the road and one could not tell where the man ended and the earth began. And I knew in my heart, the moment I was told that the man was God who was enduring all that for me, that I would not die but I would live eternally.

I went to the Oratory that day because I had known since childhood that that same man was just inside the door, actual, real.

Recently, I sat in an Ottawa home in what was a very Catholic environment and listened to a conversation between a young convert and his friend, a Catholic, in whose home the gathering was.

There was about the young convert an eagerness that was pure and filled with goodwill.

As I tuned in to their conversation, the convert was recalling the moment when he was eighteen and realized he must become a Catholic.

"It was the story of Emmaus," he said. "I was reading it and I felt the suspense as though something momentous was about to happen. They had reached the house and invited the stranger in. They sat to eat and then it happened. He broke the bread. Then he disappeared. As soon as they recognized Him he disappeared."

He looked my way then, as if realizing his audience was just increased by one.

"Into the bread," he added. "And I knew then that the thing was true. They recognized Him as they ate the bread he offered. And I knew, as of that moment, I was Catholic."

The something momentous that he had sensed approaching was within the story, yes, but outside as well. The moment would change him forever. That moment of deposit of the faith. Change him as it changes everyone who comes to know it to be true.

Alas, that is one warning the nuns never gave us and should have. They were responsible, after all, for introducing us as kids to the Blessed Sacrament. They did so simply and directly, without any talk about the "hidden God" that teachers addicted to quiz shows talk about today. They just told us about Him, then walked us across the schoolyard to the church, whispered, "There He is" and whacked us on the head if we forgot to go down on two knees. And sure enough, there He was. As real as the whack on the head. And there we were, just kids, not knowing it, but falling in love, in the only way a kid can fall in love, totally and forever.

The nuns should have warned us that we would never be the same again, that we would never get over that first meeting. They never prophesied that later on in our thirties, when we had tried out every sin more times than there are numbers to count, that when we were down and truly out, classically "fallen" and without any hope left in us, that we might pass a church in a downtown city, hear a priest intoning "This Is My Body," walk in and fall head-over-heels in love all over again.

So I walked into St. Brigid's that day, and I saw one of the Oratorian Brothers in black soutane with rosary in hand, just sitting there, doing nothing.

Oh, I don't mean he was being idle. He was looking at the Blessed Sacrament on the high altar, for it was in the monstrance and elevated to its podium atop the tabernacle. He looked startled, as though someone had just whacked him on the head. And I thought, that young man is in love.

Yet he was too young to have been taught by the nuns, the real ones. So, somehow, it happens. Introductions are made and the Blessed Sacrament has a new lover, and faithless people like myself are reminded that silly priests might savage the Church and silly nuns might dedicate themselves to Mother Earth until cows have green eyebrows but that will not stop the Mystery of Mysteries from bridging the gap and courting His creatures.

2

Mystical Visions

When the Sisters of St. Joseph were my teachers back in the '40s, a convent of seven of them stood near the school. The fact that they were solemn did not prevent them from being obvious in their happiness.

With the exception of one crank, they were very well-balanced, it appeared, and absolutely flamboyant in the way they created high drama just by walking across the schoolyard. They were aware of the authority their habits gave them and they knew how to use it. When they were in view, with their long black rosaries hanging from waist to ankle, you were absolutely certain that heaven and hell were not far away.

Those good Sisters wielded the wealth of saints in the liturgical calendar the way concert promoters herald rock stars today. Truly, they anchored the nonsense of the twentieth century to the earth so that it could not overtake impressionables such as we, in our pre-teen years. Of course there were, even among that small number of nuns, a few question marks. I still wonder about that one sister who would go on, for what seemed like hours, detailing to us the wily tricks of a totally muscular and undeniably naked Lucifer painted on a large Baltimore poster with only a few strategically painted flames to keep the girls in class from giggling.

But of the seven nuns, there was only one who could be

described as depressed. This was back, of course, before nervous breakdowns were popular and when "depression" was something that followed a stock market crash.

Recently in 1980, passing an Ottawa convent, I met two Sisters walking. I noticed without even thinking about it that they both looked not just unhappy but depressed. In thinking on it, I had to admit that in the four times I had visited their chapel that look was a constant with many of them. A good number of them are now old and in ill health. In the infirmary, one can still meet a few ancient ones with rosaries in hand. I wonder what their souls have endured since the destruction began in the '60s. I wonder if the old ones will survive that day, which cannot be far off, when the Blessed Sacrament will no longer be among them. It surely will happen, for all over Ottawa the increase in the number of priests who no longer believe in the Real Presence is alarming. One estimate puts it at 30 percent of the clergy.

The mood of the Church today is that of a loser who had it all and let it slip away. Yes, we did have it all — goodness, beauty, truth. Then the thieves went to work.

They struck Psalm 42 from the mass — "I will go unto the altar of God, to God the joy of my youth" — and never has youth had less to be joyful about than in the horror-ridden Church of today, where goodness is lost beneath scandal.

They threw out Psalm 25 — "Lord I love the beauty of thy house and the place where thy glory dwells" — and the churches of Roman Catholicism were laid waste, looted of their great art, music and architecture.

They withheld John 1:14, the most sublime wording ever to come from the mind of man — "And the Word was made Flesh ... And we saw His glory, glory as the Only Begotten of the Father, full of grace and truth" — and who can doubt that grace has been withdrawn from the Church of today, a Church daily seduced by the lie that all is well. Not all the diocese publications in the world, not all the editorials penned by bishops' secretaries, not all the glad photographs of all the happy workshopping and dialoguing committees, councils and counsellors in all of North America can alter that truth one whit.

Roman Catholicism continues hourly to be put through the shredder, as bishops pose with committee heads, council chairpersons, subcommittee co-ordinators and parish animators.

Those Sisters in the motherhouse, some of whom have had the Blessed Sacrament as their sole reason for being for eighty and ninety years, will die from its removal as surely as from old age. Yet they and we all seem so powerless to prevent that happening. It is, after all, the clergy alone, that very estate that is causing the Blessed Sacrament to disappear from tabernacles, that is capable of bringing it into our midst.

Throughout my nine childhood and teenage years as an altar boy serving mass at any and all hours of the morning, afternoon, evening or night for more priests than I can possibly recall, I never once saw or heard a priest comment upon, criticize, smirk at or mock that ingredient of worship found in all denominations and religions but notably formalized into unique behaviour in Roman Catholicism: the thoughts, words and deeds, the meditations, phrasings and gestures of human beings admitting gratitude to the Supreme Being who made all things. It is an attitude of which, out of all created life, as far as we know, only man is consciously capable — piety.

For the individual at a loss for words, the Church provided words, verses, hymns. For those shy of heart there were shadows, candles, the lit taper as it moved to find a fresh waxen wick, dispelling anew a fraction of the dark and making of the penitent an achiever. For those bursting with joy there was colour, art and, above all, architecture shouting "Author, author!" Stained glass gave eyes to the light so the saints could surround us, hold off the world and stand guard over our supplications.

In a thousand ways, Catholicism provided the means whereby the simplest heart could acclaim the sublime: the hushed, rhythmic chorus of sighs and rattling wood as beads made an abacus of fervent fingers and butternut pews. Litanies with a cadence and a rhythm that let the heart thrill anew to the names of the saints, the attributes of the Trinity, the countless ways to enumerate the Father, the Son, the Holy Ghost. The hymns to the Virgin, that constant mother of life, of sweetness and of hope. The *"Dominus Vobiscum," "Orate Fratres,"* and *"In Nomini Patris,"* that brought you momentarily face to face with the priest, that consecrated servant of God who surrendered not only his life, but also willingly offered his identity, his face, to risk looking God in the eye on our behalf. The priest, protecting his flock from that which no one has seen save the Only Begotten, preserving us lovingly at his back as Christ offered to under His wing, so that we might survive the invitation to know, to love, to serve Him in this life and be happy with Him in the next. The gesture acknowledging that greatest of truths, "And the Word was made Flesh," the genuflection, right knee to the floor alongside the left inner heel, knighthood in a gesture; the double-knee genuflection before the Blessed Sacrament, saying, as Lancelot must surely have done, "I have only one heart to give but I give it to you doubly." The linen of the communion rail that clothed in like raiment the hands of both sinner and saint. The myriad wondrous ways for the faithful to contemplate the fact that within the tabernacle, beyond that tiny door with that tiny key, just there, through that narrow gate to the faith, there beat the Heart of the One and Only Begotten of the Father.

Of all the sights, signs and symbols of Roman Catholicism, none is more touching than that tiny key in that tiny door. The faith that melted down its heart to lovingly plate in gold that tiny key was founded on one thing and one thing only — the empty tomb. The yearning, fearful human heart can get itself up to astonishing and remarkable works, but none as endearing as that gesture, like a child with his first key, trying with the clicking of a simple lock to ensure the fulfilment of the promise of He who promised that He will never leave again.

In a thousand ways, Roman Catholicism taught a language of love to hearts burning for union with the greatest of lovers. But in no word, gesture or deed did Catholicism reach the heights of eloquence that it achieved in silence. Silence, the language of love, the thunder of the heart in full storm. Silence, the mirror in which we see God.

It was everywhere. It enshrouded the sanctuary lamp flickering red like a dancing heart before the tabernacle. It

carpeted the altar as sacred vessels were placed at the ready for
mass. It crowded the confessional as the sinner disposed
himself for the first whispered blessing. It rose like waves of
unspoken *gloria*s from bank upon bank of votive candles,
flickering, sparkling, burning, all through the night and daytime
hours, dispensing always the perfect honour: silence.

It has always been so, the silence of the Church. Long
ago it caused men in the bleakest hours of the meanest age to
gather together in His name, to sing, to invent with a confidence
that forbade fear that which is called Gregorian, to empower
their voices with a thunder that would chase lightening into the
depths until the abyss was given shape and the black glow of
doubt surrendered to the stained-glass yearning of chanted
desire.

Throughout all its tormented history, Roman Catholicism
has had silence next to its heart. It is as if the silence of the
desert, in gratitude for the honour of His company, had
willingly stayed behind on earth to memorialize His forty days
of fasting.

So much a part of Catholicism was silence that it came
to mean the nearness of God. The simple act of turning off a
radio was an invitation for Him to come in, visit awhile. And
wherever, whenever, through the clanging and banging of
another day's raucous passing, a sparkle of silence broke
through, the mind turned, as if by habit, to God.

Throughout all my childhood and teenage years I never
once heard a priest, a nun or a lay person scream out in
unstoppable rage because they heard nothingness in silence.
But all along there must have been those who seethed with
hatred for these wondrous things. Who were they? Where
were they? They had no presence in Roman Catholicism as I
remember it. Yet they must have come from somewhere. How
else can we explain what has happened to all these treasures?

It is as if, through some cataclysm, the treasures of the
faith have been dropped into the waiting hands of those who
hated Roman Catholicism. The linen was torn from the
communion rail, the communion rail was torn from the floor,
the consecrated host was torn from the chalice and slapped into
the communicant's cupped hand. The tabernacle was thrown

open; untrained, unlearned, uncaring hands pawed around in there without so much as a nod or a wink of deference, and the tabernacle was left ajar, unguarded, neither coveted for what was within nor defended from what was without.

Roman Catholicism, through its language of love, offered the downtrodden, oppressed, dispirited individual countless reaffirmations of his living, breathing, one-on-one relationship with God. It nourished hope by exposing him to the idiom that is above and beyond his experience. It reinforced by its consistency the sweetness of that relationship.

Now, in its place, the language of the thing that has replaced Roman Catholicism is the language of experience only. The individual has no time to seek out his one-on-one with God. Now he is just one of a lot of other ones. He is a member of a group, a gathering, a chirping, chortling community. He must seek God there, for all the new signs tell him that God, too, is one of the group, a unit of the community. If you made all the right sounds, gave off all the right signals, flashed all the right signs, shook all the right hands, you might, by chance, shake His. Gone is the quiet of God's house. Gone the silence of inexpressible joy. Gone the silence of inexhaustible sorrow. Silence, the veil on which was imprinted the true face of Roman Catholicism, has been rent asunder to be replaced by the mask of the raucous, clanging, banging thing that has replaced it. The face of "the Church of Nothing There."

I know in my heart that the Church I love will survive somewhere, in Europe probably, in one of those countries where the cut of the land and the character of the people still reflect the mystical visions that drew countless saints from its soil in centuries past.

In Canada, we had it all, and let it slip away. And I am as guilty as the rest. I am of the generation that had it all and did nothing to preserve it.

What I and others of my generation should have done was hitch-hike to Rome the year the Second Vatican Council opened. We should have walked into the nave of St. Peter's among all those bishops and all those thieves whispering into the bishops' ears and told them they had no business stealing the mass. That it was not theirs to steal. That it was God's. And mine. I should have done all that and taken the mass back.

But I did not. Nobody did. So my generation is guilty for not being critical enough, gutsy enough to go into the Council, track down all the whispering theologians and throw them, bound and gagged, into the Tiber.

If Catholics did nothing, it was not that they did not care enough. It was, rather, that, raised to pray, obey, fill the collection plate and kiss the bishop's rings, they looked on glassy-eyed with disbelief as the sacraments were stolen from under their noses.

There are unsung sainted priests and nuns in Ottawa, serving their faithful in accordance with the promise they made when they entered religious life. The faithful have a way of finding them. The nine o'clock Sunday evening mass at St. Patrick's is always full for that very reason. Here the mass is accorded the honour and dignity that is its due.

There is something especially poignant about Catholics coming in out of the dark to that candle-lit interior on Kent Street. It is the reminder that throughout history the faithful have sought and found holiness in their midst, and by their unfailing adherence helped it to dispel the darkness.

To those priests who have resisted the corrupting trends of the archdiocese of Ottawa, history will accord Churchill's acclamation, "Never in the field of human conflict was so much owed by so many to so few."

3

What This Country Needs

Here, beside Champlain, as darkness falls over the Ottawa River, I follow his bronze gaze inland and wonder what he would say to hear that three hundred years after he opened up this country the de-Christianizing of Canada is almost complete.

Rampant consumerism, forty years without a prayer-inducing world war and the total abandonment of their vows to Christ by myriad priests and nuns of the Catholic Church have left, for the inheritors of the twenty-first century, a Canada collapsing into darkness. I venture to say that the one sure ingredient other Christian denominations gained from collaborating with Catholics in the hollow ecumenism that followed Vatican II was the certainty that they, too, would lose focus and crumble into confusion. But I cannot speak for them. I am a Roman Catholic first and only, and if I have anywhere here offended or shown disrespect for other denominations of Christianity and other religions, I sincerely beg their forgiveness.

You can love Catholicism or you can hate it, but our heritage as a country is one that began with ripples of the faith from Catholic France washing up against the shores of the St. Lawrence. When Jacques Cartier planted a thirty-foot wooden

cross on the shores of Chaleur Bay on July 24, 1534, he also
planted the will to survive. Those early pioneers founded
institutions in health, education and commerce so well grounded
that even after the French went down to defeat at the Plains of
Abraham in 1759, the British left them in place and provided
for their security. Canada, as we know it, resulted from what
occurred in Quebec and Montreal in the few short months
following Montcalm's fall.

I see this once-great country, blessed above all other
countries on earth, falling on its face because we have not
honoured our past, our beginnings, our heritage, just as the
post-Vatican II Church is already on its hands and knees and
belly and face because it adamantly refuses to acknowledge
the value of the desperately needed order that existed before
1960.

Early morning. Cock-crow hour. A full moon over the
statue of Champlain. Looking south from the point, one sees
the step locks at the Rideau Canal descending to the Ottawa
River. Above the trees shifting restlessly in silhouette is a
shadow that does not move; it is the Angel of Victory stepping
skyward from the arch above the war memorial.

Come here to take the pulse of my country, where the life
blood of this land flows past bronzed victims forever parading
in victory over death. Come here to see the contradictions
dancing in the moonlight, the moment, arrested for all to share,
when man overcomes chaos and that other endless stream, an
unstoppable, desirable vein of future times risking chaos all
over again.

Come here to wonder at this country, barely formed,
being scissored, severed, ripped and shredded. Come here to
sense the loss. We are dismembered, because we did not love
all this enough to bring it to term.

The whole has been shattered, strength and unity
dispersed. The beauty of clear purpose is gone. The beauty of
gracious behaviour, gone. The sense of the sacred, all gone
from this once-blessed land.

Is it too late for all we were, all we dreamed, all we
believed? Is it too late to salvage for others yet to come the

unutterable beauty of what we have, the soul of this great country? It is a soul so intensely rich that the human spirit is compelled to cry out in astonishment at its purity, to utter *mea culpa*s unexpectedly one day as the Cabot Trail beneath our feet romances us and has its way, or to cock an ear and try to hear what sounds just like *"Laudamus Dei"* as blizzards roar up Matapédia, to St. Lawrence and Lévis.

My dear Champlain, is it too late?

I ache for the Church I love and country whose survival I crave. Today I can scarcely separate the beauty there once was in each, for I have dreamed long into the night with both.

I have heard the *Agnus Dei* played on fiddles in Gaspé. I have heard a tundra choir warm to Latin as to fire. I have seen *"in excelsis deo,"* sung in high Cree nasal wail, hang like carpets of wintry light in the blue-black northern sky to dance, to tease, to mystify. And children of the wheat fields sing, as prairie angels surely must, *"et in terra pax hominibus."*

And once, as the wheels of CP Rail rocked out *"Credo in unum Deum,"* I read that Riel's final sigh was a whispered *"pleine de grâce"*.

Oh, my dear Champlain, can you not see? What this country needs is Christmas, and the truth of the Incarnation brought home to it once more. Were it not for Christmas, children today would have little or no knowledge of a loving God.

For those who have endured the decades that have passed since New Year's Day 1960 and survived with their faith more or less intact, a strong sense of Christmas may have fortified them sufficiently to escape the fate of so many other Catholics, who watched as the fruit of the Incarnation, the great sacrifice that is the mass, became first a banquet and then a fast-food charade.

Until Christmas is outlawed, or worse, becomes the subject of a parish council, there is at least some hope that the Incarnation will reach a child's heart. It is the one story teachers can tell any day of the year; children will love it and contribute to it. If a teacher had nothing else when he entered his profession but a red pencil for marking papers and the ability to tell the Christmas story, he would be equipped to govern in the holy place the child's house of learning should be. That, and the good luck to have a robin land on the window-sill.

"Teacher, why does the robin have a red breast?"

"Because he was the only bird flying over the garden at the moment of the Resurrection."

"What's a Resurrection?"

"Child, do I have a story for you!"

4

Litany

No one knows what Champlain really looked like. The earliest portrait, from which his familiar likeness was initially established and over the centuries reproduced for statues, school books and plaques, was apparently not of him at all. So we are not even certain that he wore the great moustache and goatee that magnifies the handsome visage on the statue on Nepean Point. But all that does not really matter. I know what he looks like. Every schoolboy knows his eyes are squinted from holding his astrolabe up to the sky. His skin is toughened by sea wind and log fires. His stance is erect, dignified, commanding. And his fingernails are clean, because he was a prayerful man and it is hard to keep hands pressed together for a *Pater Noster*, an *Ave* or a *Gloria* if you can see that your nails are dirty.

His king knew what he looked like. His wife Hélène knew. The men he commanded knew. And the Indians knew. Now, in Quebec, as they have for the past few years, archaeologists continue to dig feverishly to identify his grave, coffin and body. How, one wonders, will they know him if he has not named his coffin? What will Quebec nationalists do if they discover that, far from looking like the Champlain of the public squares and history books, his remains suggest he looked like, say, Mark Twain or Charles Dickens or Robert Louis Stevenson?

I have chosen not to identify by name the priests and Brothers who were the Oratorians, with the exception of Father Ashley, whose comments being included here made it proper and necessary, and Father Donald Neilson whose privacy now cannot be invaded. My reason is that they themselves would acknowledge that they, individually, were not the story. Their vision was the story and, as with every action, word and service they performed for the faithful they shepherded for two years, they here decrease so their vision might increase.

Their identity is known in a litany of ways.

Those who received the sacraments from them know their name.

Those who were transfixed by their glorious masses know their name.

Those who thought them good men know their name.

Those who thought them less than perfect know their name.

Those who took up petitions against them know their name.

Those who slandered, libelled and calumniated them know their name.

The faithful they are serving now in their various far-flung locations all know their name.

Those priests on the priests' council who could not wait to get them out of the archdiocese, the detested clique who controlled the archbishop's infamous *Church in Ottawa Today* publication, the jackbooting nuns and the archbishop's pitiable secretary who orchestrated so much of the opposition against them, and Joseph Aurèle Plourde, they all no doubt will never forget their name.

Liberamus Domino!

5

In The Shadow Of The Valois

They used to say, those Irish and French who lived along the Ottawa, that if you lived within earshot of the bell in Notre Dame you would never be bitter in this life. For that reason Louis Riel, no doubt, went up to the choir loft in the basilica on his illicit, secret visit to Ottawa a few short years before he was hanged. It houses so much of our heritage. If you want to know Riel, go there, into the choir gallery, and see and hear what he did.

Among the treasures of the basilica now not in view are the complete mortal remains of St. Felicity, brought from Rome around the time of the potato famine in Ireland.[1] The certainty of which St. Felicity it may be is hidden with her bones, but I hope it is she who, before walking into the arena, exchanged the true kiss of peace with her fellow martyrs.[2] One kiss from her would repair the hollow mockery of airborne cocktail kisses that smack through the air of our Sunday romps now.

To the left of the altar of the Sacred Heart hangs an exquisite life-sized crucifix carved by the artist Dauphin.

Today, when the cross itself, let alone the Corpus, is

banished from Catholic churches, this gripping image, in all its tortured nakedness, makes the blood stop in the veins of the onlooker. Here is a powerful man, big-boned and muscular, like the Irishmen and Frenchmen who timber-rafted down the Ottawa River. The body is fastened with immovable spikes to squared beams, low to the floor, the cross holds the body firmly. The weight of those human limbs might even pull free, but within this special body there is a force stronger than the pull of freedom, a need greater then the need for rest. The hands, the feet, grotesquely abused, seem to covet the nails that hold them to the lumber.

The head is down to conceal something in the face. It is not the collapsed neck of death, though the great ragged wound from the lance has already emptied blood and water from the side. There is something purposeful, willed, in the angle of the face. At first the source of the mystery eludes the eye. Then it is there, startlingly close. It is in the lips, pursed as if in one last sip of breath, or one last whisper of a name. Whose name? Could we bear to hear those lips call out our name? Probably not. The sculptor knew that, so he helped his helpless subject avert our eye by carving in death a glance that turns away.

Also in the basilica somewhere, although they do not like to let on about it any more, is the elbow of St. Victor.

I am not one of those who advocate that since the dead do not use their elbows we can do whatever we want with them. The dispersion of fingers, forearms, thighbones and whatnot of people who were notably good before they were notably dead has always struck me as sensationally curious and curiously sensational. But since visiting the tombs of saints and heroes has been the highlight of much of man's travels, I can empathize with the faithful who, unable to afford pilgrimages, nevertheless crave to hinge themselves to some remnant of proven goodness. After all, there seems so little of it about.

No single work in the basilica, however, has held my affections more than the Golden Madonna. She stands atop the tabernacle on the altar of the Immaculate Conception, a stout little maiden eighteen inches high. Often in the year of persecution of the Oratorians I would return here to the basilica to visit the Golden Madonna and muse over that time in our faith when the Virgin was so loved. Other times the bizarre goings-on in the post-Vatican II Church would reduce me to sitting numb in the pew playing mental hockey with St. Victor's elbow.

Over a hundred years ago, in an act of devotion for which the French and Irish of Lowertown are rightly famous, the women of the parish melted down their jewellery to completely cover the Virgin in a layer of warm, glowing gold.

Was that only a century ago? It seems several millennia removed from the world of Canada's capital city archdiocese today, where a hideous, Church-sanctioned insult to the Mother of God is repeated with calculated precision each month, on the same day, at the same hour, at the same location.

Throughout the two years the Oratorians served in Ottawa, they conducted on the thirteenth of each month Our Lady's Oratory, an evening service consisting of benediction and fifteen decades of the rosary in honour of the request made by Our Lady of Fatima in Portugal in 1917.

On the thirteenth of the first month following the Oratorians' expulsion, the doors of St. Brigid's were found to be locked when the faithful, now without their priests, showed up to continue their devotions. The priest replacement, Father Harold MacNeil, has refused to open it to this day.[3] For over two years now, at the time of this writing, the faithful have stood outside the locked doors of St. Brigid's on the thirteenth of each month in rain, in snow, in raw and fickle Ottawa weather to continue keeping their Fatima promise with candles, rosaries and hymns. There they have been found each month, a core remnant of the numbers who flocked weekly to the Oratory, proving unmistakably that the Oratorians, far from imposing "outdated pre-Vatican II spirituality" on their flock, were, in fact, responding to the aspirations of a congregation who saw nothing outmoded in honouring the Mother of God.

Plourde claimed on the technicality of incardination that there never had been an Oratory in Ottawa. Well, in reality, there had. Undying faith has a spectacular habit of dispensing with technicalities

I believe that if you go to St. Brigid's on the thirteenth of the month to see this phenomenon of the faith in action you will find the Mother of God, not behind the locked doors, but there, in their midst, upright among them, silent, stoic, steadfast, the *Stabat Mater*, by her presence adding her strength to theirs. For these are the same faithful who knelt in the Cova da Iria in Fatima in 1917 and saw the sun fall spinning from the sky, the same faithful whose prayers raised on Montmartre the great Sacre Coeur to atone for the massacre of priests during the communard, the same faithful who turned prayerfully toward Rome when Pius IX was reduced to landlessness by the Piedmontese, the same faithful who lost their priests in the September Massacre of 1792. And, I believe, she stood with them, by the Cross her station keeping, on October 7, 1571, when the rosary overcame the Turks at Lepanto while "the shadow of the Valois is yawning" was "the mass."[4]

6

Lavabo

Among the innocent lives the certainty that Justice will have the last word. The last word? Is it that time already? Is it too late to direct the Church back to the truth of the Incarnation? With the priesthood levelled, to whom would the task be entrusted?

Alas, it is upon the laity that the fate of the Church now rests. Their little acts of loyalty to the Pope must substitute for the act of loyalty the bishops refuse to give him. Only an act of unconditional loyalty to the Holy Father can sustain Roman Catholicism in Canada. We will not know what act of loyalty to commit until we have reached our breaking point and see a point of no return just there ahead of us.

For me, the point of no return came in 1975. An impulse to do something to restore some part of the Church compelled me to gather up the sacred vestments once borrowed from a church for a theatrical event about Joan of Arc. There were albs and chasubles and capes and copes and stoles and amulets in green and silver and gold, heavy with rich brocade. To return them to the church across the province from which they came, I bought a second-hand car from an anthropologist and left Toronto heading west toward Sarnia and the border crossing at St. Mary's. I crossed over into Michigan easily enough, but when I reached the Sault Ste. Marie International

Bridge for a crossing back into Canada, Customs officials were more demanding. While I told one official my point of origin and my destination, another went to the rear of the car and opened the trunk. He muttered, rummaged around, then called out to his partner.

"Hey, this guy's got the whole College of Cardinals in here."

It seems he'd uncovered what I had not even noticed; in the wheel hollow of the trunk, beneath the mounds of church vestments, was a carton of human bones.

It took eight hours for them to determine that the bones were two hundred years old but just one glance to tell me two things I should have already known.

One, never buy a used car from an anthropologist.

Two, the discarded vestments and the carton of dry bones made an all-too-accurate depiction of the state of the Church I loved so dearly. The cauldron was brimming with brocade and bone but no one remembered the recipe for the stew.

We must remember: it is our very heritage as well as our faith that is at stake. We must find the means to save what is our birthright. If not we, then who will do it for us? Must it be left to others to do? Must we hope that immigrants to this great land will love it more than we and determine on ways to save it for us? Will they see what we see? Save what we would save?

When Montcalm fell and New France was signed away to the British with a flurry of ostrich quills and wrist ruffles in Versailles, the English charted the Ottawa River anew, removed the saints' names from their places of honour along the Ottawa and substituted for them such awe-inspiring place names as Sandy Beach, Sandy Point, Black Bay and White Lake. Thus the saints vanished from the river, with the notable exceptions of St. Anne and St. Joachim, who have a way of staying on when lesser saints yield to the pressures and prejudices of the times.

So where did they go, these saints who were so unceremoniously dislodged? Did they fade into the forest?

Assume themselves into the folklore of the Indians? Shadow the English as they laid claim to the interior? Or were they swept downriver to the habitations of those sons and daughters of France who had brought them to the new world?

I can tell you, because I found them, on the first Friday of Advent, 1988.

On that day, three wise men followed my lead into the city of Montreal in search of treasure. These were not *the* three wise men, nor do I mean to imply that in following me they were following anything remotely resembling an other-world brilliance of whatever wattage. Certainly that early Friday morning as we headed out of Ottawa into wet snow and pelting rain, I was a burnt-out meteorite who had thudded to earth more times than I care to recount. I call them wise because, in spite of their ages — twenty, sixteen and twenty four — they spoke openly that day of the present grief in Roman Catholicism, the loss of beauty, of unity, of certainty since Vatican II. Not one of them knew the Church before 1960, yet they had made the grief of the Church their own.

The treasure sought in Montreal was the mountain of altar vessels, fixtures, statues, crucifixes, chandeliers, candelabra and whatnot that we thought must certainly exist there, where the dismantling of such accessories of kingship had been conducted at a steady pace since 1960. Not since Pizarro set the ransom for the Atahuallapa had men's minds been so focused on finding a room piled high with treasure.

We found nothing. All evidence of the glory that once was the sanctuary of the Most High God in Quebec had simply disappeared. In churches laid bare by Vatican II grey-paint enthusiasts, there was scarcely a memory of the accoutrements of worship. After all, years had passed since that first day when a Catholic, slipping into a candle-lit early morning church in search of the tabernacle and majesty, found himself meditating instead on the fabric of a presider's chair.

Late in the day we found ourselves in a shop on Papineau Street where my companions made inquiries about the cost of statuary. We were conducted into a back room. And there they were, every saint I had every prayed to, some fresh out of their moulds — St. Teresa, St. Margaret, St. Anthony, and on and on. Above all of them towered the statue of St. Joseph, the Child Jesus held to his chest. "The Church is safe in his arms but he is taking it into Egypt for awhile," was the thought that flashed to mind.

In the corner, near the wall, stood a tall wooden statue of Mary, from Italy. The statue had no hands, just sockets at the ends of each sleeve where hands should have been. This image was more than upsetting.

Mary was the original tabernacle of the Blessed Sacrament. Though she had been shuffled off out of the post-conciliar Church just as surely as tabernacles had been sidelined, still, there was always the sense of her authority, her ability to save the feast, to get the water turned into wine. But to see her without hands? All the saints that ever were could be washed away down every river in Christendom, but to see Mary debilitated, limited, was simply too much.

On the way out of the back room, trying to get away from that disturbing sight, I glanced back. What I experienced then was one of those unique moments that come unheralded into our lives and set us on journeys of the heart we never dreamed we would take. Glancing back, I saw that the sockets of Mary's sleeves were hidden by two of my three companions. They were standing quite still looking at the face of the statue.

The tableau held for only an instant, yet it etched its imprint deep into my presumptions about the fate of the Church. All the way home, as snow pelted the windshield and the tires rolled on through endless ridges of November slush, I kept thinking of the Fatima message, that the twentieth century had been placed in Mary's hands. These young men were her hands.

The true priests and true nuns, those who have not yielded to the pressures and prejudices of these sad and silly times, will soon be swept away by age, their roles as Father, Sister, Brother relabelled with such confidence-eroding titles as presider, conciliator, facilitator. And all memory, all trace of their goodness, service, the litany of holiness that was their lives will vanish like those saints along the Ottawa River so long ago.

The youth of this world, with all their demands, insist on

justice. That is what rebellion is all about. But that other yearning, for which youth is renowned and upon which the world has been dependant since its creation, is the one that will rescue the church — that yearning for beauty, goodness, truth.

As if to confirm my guess, a conversation began between the two in the back seat. The discussion was on the Shroud of Turin, how science was about to announce whether or not carbon-dating would prove that it was the burial cloth of Christ.

The conversation turned to the man on the shroud. There was much talk about the burial position, the side wound, the marks of the scourging, the crown of thorn wounds. Then the younger of the two, the sixteen-year-old said, "He sure has big shoulders."

He was not speaking metaphorically, he meant the shoulders of the man on the shroud were literally broad. Yet something in the saying of it banished winter, changed November to springtime, melted ice and started the water trickling once more into crevices and gullies and meadows. The deer once more would have a running stream.

It was the intimacy in his voice. Not only the fact that he would say it, but the way in which he said it, with certainty, confidence and reverence, yet with that same relentless boyishness that allows altar boys on their knees before the Blessed Sacrament to yawn languorously without the least hesitation . That innocent friendliness toward the Divine–that is Roman Catholicism at its purest. For a moment, we were all back where we belonged, at the altar of God, the joy of our youth.

"He sure has big shoulders," he said lovingly, as if that particular boy had made the discovery while in adoration before the Blessed Sacrament. For all I know, maybe he had.

He may very well be the last Roman Catholic in Canada by the time you read this. There may be other Roman Catholics left in other countries. There may even be other Roman Catholics left in Canada. But chances are that if you are reading this somewhere within Canada then you are in an archive and it is twenty years later, and if it should happen that there is a full moon tonight, think how lucky you are to not be

in Ottawa, for on such a night at cock-crow hour the Club Med
Fathers and Romper Room Valkyries will all be out at Major's
Hill Park dancing around the oak and swooning in front of the
Big Acorn.

I do most certainly hope, if it is twenty years later, the
world did not turn out to be as frightful as it promised back in
the 1990s

That was the decade the faith of our fathers vanished
from my country.

Epilogue

Ite Missa Est

Martyrs never seem to be in a hurry. The Oratorians' last mass with full choir took place on Sunday, June 25, 1989. They would linger on, reduced in many ways, until August 15. That day following farewells, a handful of the bereaved faithful conducted a wake for the faith in Ottawa led by four people in black mourning attire. They walked the six hundred and fifty paces from St. Brigid's to the archbishop's palace and laid at his door a black wreath. It signified the death of a brilliant revival of Roman Catholicism but it was, alas, also emblematic of a bleak judgment. That black circular graphic against the archbishop's door represented the only empty numeral, zero, the worst answer a shepherd could give to the question "What did you feed my sheep? What did you feed my lambs ?"

Soon after, out of that same small group of mourners would come the founders of *The Orator*, a publication totally free of archdiocesan interference, a counterweight to the vanity sheet published by the archbishop's office and a crystal clear voice of orthodoxy now speaking out from the capital of Canada to all of North America.

Once the Oratorians were gone, their jubilant opponents rushed into the vacuum of St. Brigid's to an empty triumph. Neither time nor the very best of archdiocesan public relations have been able to fill the vacuum. In a sad and pathetic acknowledgement of the hollowness of their victory the bewildered mod squad now running St. Brigid's have mounted an effort to try and simulate something of what was lost.

The result confirms their complete inability to comprehend why people drove fifty miles to worship here from 1987 to 1989. In the same church where each and every Sunday during the Oratorians tenure the Blessed Sacrament was exposed all day for adoration you will now find, as announced on a poster for June 2, 1991:

"Music for a Sunday afternoon. Works for voice and organ. Bach, Handel, Mozart, Haydn, Shubert, Chopin, Irish folk, Negro spiritual, Gershwin. "

I had intended June 25 to be my last mass there. I could not go back. I did not have the stomach to watch them endure their diminishment any longer. Yet something brought me to the door on August 15. Just as the farewell mass ended, so my last memory of the Oratory is close, immediate.

The altar quietens. Clouds of incense fade back to where mists come from. The altar boys, nearby, in the aisle, are quickly proceeding toward their exit, returning to earth's orbit, the ancient floors revealing that they are once again subject to the force of gravity.

Pews creak, doors swing open, the church empties; I am once again on the street. Soon, I know, I must reach my pencil to the sky and join the dots to reread the designs of heaven, for like the unsoldiered hand that cannot sustain a fist, the soul at middle age cannot for long play host to the joy of God. It will take another act of worship to bring Him back. I want to bring Him back. For I want to know some certainties again, and only in that particle of holy time, in an act of reverence to someone greater than myself, is it possible to see what children know — that stars are rings on angels' toes, and fireflies, beatitudes looking for a home. That thunder is an echo of the opening tomb, and moonlight is a memory of treasure on the moon before they painted it grey.

To The Nine Who
Came From The West

Your rhythm of heart beating for God

Made my heart beat faster.

Now adrift in the sky, a balloon on a string

It beats all alone in the wild.

God grant a fair breeze will carry me where

She is gathering gifts for her Child.

Notes

Part I - The Altar Of God

1. Saints Along The River

1. Coulson, John, *The Saints* (New York:Hawthorne Books Inc., 1958)

2. Ibid.

3. *Parish Notes*, St. Brigid's 50th Commemorative Issue, 1939.

4. Lefebvre, Archbishop Marcel, Sermon delivered 1976, Re: " Documentation Catholique". April 4, 1965.

5. Lemius, J.B., OMI, *A Catechism of Modernism* (Rockford, Illinois: Tan Books and Publishers Inc., 1981).

2. Tradition Has It

1. Murphy, Francis X., C.S.S.R., *The Papacy Today* (New York: MacMillan, 1981), 15.

2. Hibbert Christopher, *The French Revolution* (London: Allen Lane Publishers, 1980).

3. Holmes, Derek J., *The Papacy in the Modern World,* (New York: Crossroad Publishers, 1981).

4. Lipson E., *Europe in the Nineteeth Century* (London:A&C Black, 1916).

5. Holmes, *The Papacy in the Modern World.*

6. Murphy, *The Papacy Today.*

7. Ibid, 33.

8. Ibid.

9. McCormack, Anne O'Hare, *Vatican Journal (1921-59),* (New York: Farrar, Straus and Cudahy, 1957).

10. Ibid.

11. Bell, George, *Inside the Vatican,* (London, Hutchison, 1882).

12. Ibid.

13. Ibid.

14. Ibid.

15. Murphy, *The Papacy Today,* 15.

16. McCormack, *Vatican Journal (1921-59),* 111.

17. Ibid.

18. Ibid.

19. Murphy, Francis, *The Papacy Today,* 15.

3. The Persuaders

1. Hebblethwaite, Peter, *In the Vatican* (London: Sidgwick & Jackson, 1986).

2. Ibid.

3. Ibid.

4. Ibid.

5. Ibid.

6. Holmes, Derek J., *The Papacy in the Modern World* (New York: Crossroad Publisher, 1981).

7. Lemius, J.B., OMI, *A Catechism of Modernism* (Rockford, Illinois: Tan Books and Publishers Inc., 1981).

8. Ibid.

9. Murphy, Francis X., C.S.S.R., *The Papacy Today* (New York: MacMillan, 1981), 15.

10. Hebblethwaite, *In the Vatican*, 37.

11. Holmes, *The Papacy in the Modern World*, 228.

12. Hebblethwaite, *In the Vatican*, 37.

13. Foy, Msgr. Vincent N., "Tragedy at Winnipeg," *Human Life International* (Gaithesburg, reprint 13).

14. Ibid, 36.

Part II - The Altar Of Man

1. Bonfires

1. MacEachern, Michael, *The Orator* vol.1, no. 1, July/August 1990

Part III - The Oratorian Affair

1. Romanesque Victorian Gothic Ironic

1. *Parish Notes*, St. Brigid's 50th Commemorative Issue, 1939.

2. "Restoring The Sacred," Video Reference to Ontario Heritage Foundation, Ministry of Culture & Communication Classification, Sacred Heritage Production, November, 1989.

3. Ibid.

4. Gard, Arson, *The Hub and the Spoke* (Ottawa: Emerson Press, 1904).

5. Ibid.

6. Bond, Courtney, *Where Rivers Meet* (Woodlands Hills, California: Windsor Publication, 1984).

7. "Restoring The Sacred", Video interview with Brother Philip Hannis, Sacred Heritage Productions, November, 1989.

8. Galles, Duane, "For All the Saints, the Ottawa Tradition", *Sacred Music* vol.115. no.4, Winter 1988.

9. Byfield, Virginia, "Does Anybody Want an Oratory?" *The Western Report*, 1989.

10. Ashley, Father William, "The Last Mass," Video interview, July 1989.

2. Invitation To A Theme Park

1. Letters from the Office of Archbishop Aurèle J. Plourde, Ottawa, August 5, 1986.

2. Coulson, John, Ed. *The Saints* (New York: Hawthorne Books, Inc., 1958).

3. Ashley, Father William, "The Last Mass," Video interview, July 1989.

4. Byfield, Virginia, "Does Anybody Want an Oratory?" *The Western Report*, 1986.

3. The Golden Boot Award

1. Coulson, John, Ed. *The Saints* (New York: Hawthorne Books, Inc., 1958).

2. Letters from the Office of Archbishop Aurèle J. Plourde, Ottawa, August 5 1986.

3. Byfield, Virginia, "Does Anybody Want an Oratory?" *The Western Report*, 1989.

4. Something Franciscan

1. Ravier, André, S.J. *Bernadette* (London: Collins, 1978).

2. Ibid.

3. Letters from the Office of Archbishop J. Aurèle Plourde, Ottawa, November 9, 1987.

4. Powers, Rev. Patrick, *The Church in Ottawa Today*, 1989.

5. Plourde, Archbishop, J. Aurèle, *The Information Bulletin*, June, 1989.

6. Ibid.

7. MacEachern, Sylvia, "Unholy Alliance", *The Orator*, vol. 1, no.2, September/October 1990.

5. A Night At The Opera

1. Plourde, Archbishop J.Aurèle, *Information Bulletin*, June, 1989

2. Ashley, Rev. William, "The Last Mass," Audio interview, July, 1989.

3. Ibid.

4. Plourde, Archbishop J. Aurèle, enclosure with letter from the Archbishop, 20 September 1987.

5. Ibid.

6. Letter to Archbishop Plourde, 9 November 1987.

7. Letter to Archbishop Plourde, date concealed.

8. Letter to Archbishop Plourde, 9 November 1987.

9. Letter to Archbishop Plourde, date concealed.

10. Plourde, Archbishop J. Aurèle, enclosure with letter from the Archbishop Plourde, 20 September 1987.

11. Ibid.

12. Ibid.

13. Ibid.

14. Letter to Archbishop Plourde, 9 November 1987.

6. Dialogue Of The Oratorians

1. Letter, dated 7 January 1988, *Information Bulletin*.

2. Ibid.

3. Letter, dated 21 September 1987, *Information Bulletin*.

4. Ibid.

5. Ashley, Rev. William, "The Last Mass," Audio interview, July 1989.

6. Letter, dated 21 September 1987, *Information Bulletin*, June 1989.

7. Ibid.

8. Ibid.

9. Ashley, Rev. William, "The Last Mass," Audio interview, July 1989.

10. Letter, dated 21 September 1987, *Information Bulletin,* June, 1989.

11. Ibid.

12. U.S. Catholic Conference, "Environment and Art in Catholic Worship." (Washington: 1987).

13. Letter, dated 21 September 1987, *Information Bulletin,* June 1989

14. Ashley, Rev. William, "The Last Mass," Audio interview, July 1989.

15. Letter, dated 21 September 1987, *Information Bulletin,* June 1989.

16. Letter, dated 7 January 1988, *Information Bulletin* , June 1989.

17. Ibid.

18. Ibid.

19. Letter, dated 7 January 1988, *Information Bulletin* , June, 1989.

20. Ibid.

21. Liturgy Documentary Series "General Instruction on the Roman Missal," (Washington: U.S. Catholic Conference, 1970).

22. Ibid.

23. Letter, dated 21 September 1987, *Information Bulletin,* June 1989

24. Letter , dated 4 December 198, *Information Bulletin* , June 1989.

25. *Parish Notes,* St. Brigid's 50th Commemorative Issue, 1939.

26. Letter, dated 7 January 1988, *Information Bulletin* , June 1989.

27. Ibid.

28. Ibid.

29. Plourde, Archbishop J. Aurèle, *Information Bulletin,* June 1989.

30. Ibid.

31. Letter, dated 7 January 1988, *Information Bulletin,* June 1989.

32. Ibid.

7. Latch-keys

1."Open Letter to Archbishop Plourde," 7.

2. Ratzinger, Cardinal, *The Ratzinger Report,* with Vittorio Messori, (San Francisco: Ignatius Press 1984).

3. MacDonald, Bishop, *The Canadian League,* February 1989.

4. *The Northwestern Ontario Catholic* , March 1989.

5. MacEachern, Sylvia, "Unholy Alliance," *The Orator* , vol. 1 no. 2, September/October 1990.

6. MacEachern, Sylvia, "Dignity – Perversion Tolerated," *The Orator*, Vol. 1, no. 1, July/August 1990.

7. Ibid.

8. Hardon, John A., *Treasury of Catholic Wisdom* , (New York: Doubleday, 1987), 659.

9. Plourde, Archbishop J. Aurèle *Information Bulletin* , June 1989.

10.Ibid, 6.

11.Ibid.

8. Eviction

1. Plourde, Archbishop J. Aurele, *Information Bulletin*, June 1989.

2. Ashley, Rev. William, "The Last Mass," Audio interview, July 1989

3. Ibid.

4. Coulson, John, Ed., *The Saints* (New York: Hawthorne Books Inc., 1958)

Part IV - Thieves At The Altar

1. Vatican Valkyries

1. Lemius. J.B., OMI, *A Catechism of Modernism* (Rockford, Illinois: Tan Books and Publishers, Inc., 1981).

2. Ibid.

3. Ibid.

4. Ibid.

5. Ibid.

6. Ibid.

7. Ibid.

8. Kelly, Mgr. George A., *The Battle For The American Church* (New York: Doubleday, 1979).

2. Thieves

1. Letter, dated 7 January 1988, *Information Bulletin*, June 1989.

2. Bond, Courtney, *City On The Ottawa*, (Ministry of Public Works, 1965).

Part V - Among The Innocent

5. In The Shadow Of The Valois

1. Coulson, John, Ed. *The Saints* (New York: Hawthorne Books Inc., 1958).
2. Ibid.
3. Scanlon, David, "Closed Church Draws Prayer Protest" *Ottawa Citizen*, 14 October 1989.
4. Chesteron, G.K. " Lepanto" poem, *The Eye Witness* (London: H. Belloc & C. Chesterton Publishers, October 12, 1911).

Further References

Abbott, Walter M., S.J. Ed., *The Documents of Vatican II* (Herder and Herder Association Press, 1966).

Cheetham, Nicholas. *Keeper of the Keys* (New York: Scribner 1983).

Constitution on Sacred Liturgy (Boston:Daughters of Saint Paul, 1963).

Documents of Vatican II (Grand Rapids: Erdmans, 1975).

Instruction on the Liturgy (Boston: Daughters of Saint Paul, 1968).

Johnson, Paul. *Pope John Paul II and the Catholic Restoration* (London: Weidenfeld and Nicolson, 1985).

Martin, Malachi. *The Decline and Fall of The Roman Church* (New York: Putnam, 1981).

Martin, Malachi. *The Keys of This Blood* (New York: Simon & Shuster, 1990).

Muggeridge, Anne Roche. *Desolate City* (Toronto: McClelland Stewart, 1986).

Nicols, Peter. *The Pope's Divisions* (Toronto: Clarke Irwin & Co. Ltd., 1981).

Thomas, Gordon. and Max Morgan Witts. *Pontiff* (London: Granada 1983).

For Notre Dame Interior, see Pagé, Normal, *La Cathedral Notre Dame d'Ottawa* (Ottawa: University of Ottawa Press, 1988).